ELIAS MUNSHYA
Barrister & Solicitor

Proclaiming
Political Pluralism

Recent Titles in
Religion in the Age of Transformation

Proclaiming Political Pluralism

Churches and Political Transitions in Africa

Isaac Phiri

ELIAS MUNSHYA
Barrister & Solicitor

Religion in the Age of Transformation
Anson Shupe, Series Adviser

PRAEGER

Westport, Connecticut
London

Library of Congress Cataloging-in-Publication Data

Phiri, Isaac, 1962–
  Proclaiming political pluralism : churches and political transitions in Africa / Isaac Phiri.
    p. cm.—(Religion in the age of transformation, ISSN 1087–2388)
  Includes bibliographical references and index.
  ISBN 0–275–97214–3 (alk. paper)
  1. Christianity and politics—Africa, Sub-Saharan—History—20th century. 2. Church and
state—Africa, Sub-Saharan—History—20th century. 3. Africa, Sub-Saharan—Politics and
government—1960– 4. Africa, Sub-Saharan—Church history—20th century. I. Title. II.
Series.
  BR1430.P47 2001
  261.7′0968—dc21   2001021170

British Library Cataloguing in Publication Data is available.

Library of Congress Catalog Card Number: 2001021170
ISBN: 0–275–97214–3
ISSN: 1087–2388

First published in 2001

Praeger Publishers, 88 Post Road West, Westport, CT 06881
An imprint of Greenwood Publishing Group, Inc.
www.praeger.com

Printed in the United States of America

∞™

The paper used in this book complies with the
Permanent Paper Standard issued by the National
Information Standards Organization (Z39.48–1984).

10 9 8 7 6 5 4 3 2 1

To my wife, Dora, my son Basil, and my daughter, Monica.

Contents

Acknowledgments

I am most grateful to acquisitions editor Suzanne I. Staszak-Silva for her encouraging and helpful input in conceptualizing the scope of this project. I am also indebted to Patricia Porco and other detail-oriented production editors at Greenwood for helping to make this a more readable and accurate work. Suzanne, Patricia, and other behind-the-scenes editorial staff at Greenwood have helped make this a stronger and better work.

This study has been in the works for several years. I am therefore hesitant to name people as I will most certainly omit individuals who might have been most encouraging at some point in the development of the book. However, I feel obligated to mention some professors at Northern Illinois University. Professor Daniel Kempton, chair of the Department of Political Science, helped me think through substantive ideas contained in this book from its conception. Thanks also to Professor Gary Glen for forcing me to think even harder on questions concerning the interface of religion and politics. Professor Greg Schmidt's expansive understanding of Latin American politics provided illuminating comparative insights to my interest in church-state issues in Africa. Professor Ferald Bryan stimulated my interest in the efficacy of religious rhetoric in national and international politics.

Numerous other people have helped make this book what it is. A number of colleagues from South Africa and Zimbabwe read through early drafts of chapters on these countries and came back with affirming comments. My thanks also go to Richard Sakala, President Frederick Chiluba's press assistant, who helped make possible a personal interview with the Zambian head of state on matters of church-state. The chapter on Zambia would not have been the same without the personal interview with President Chiluba.

I have to stop somewhere. Many have helped make this a better book but I remain responsible for any weaknesses and shortfalls.

Chapter One ———————————————————————

Churches and the African
Political Arena

This book is prompted by the visible role that the churches played in the African transitions to plural politics in the 1990s and explores why and how churches were drawn into this role, which invariably brought them into direct confrontation with the political establishment.[1] This is a pervasive and important phenomenon in African politics: the tendency of churches to episodically enter the political arena and assume a critical role when all other elements of civil society face severe repression.[2] The central argument of the work is that this episodic intervention of churches into national politics is linked to the vacuum that occurs in African political systems, resulting from state repression of civil society.[3]

The book shows that churches often confront the state when a predatory government has pulverized civil society groups that would otherwise play this role. Once civil society is liberated, the churches tend to withdraw from the political arena to their less visible and more traditional pastoral functions. The pattern is illuminated by comparing and contrasting the roles churches have played in the politics of Zambia, Zimbabwe, South Africa, and other sub-Saharan countries.

The value of understanding the dynamics that draw African churches into the political arena cannot be overstated. Anson Shupe and Jeffrey K. Hadden observed that "The prospect of finding . . . patterns among the seemingly diverse ways in which religion and the social order interface is a challenge of the first order for the social sciences."[4] This work contributes to an understanding of the interface between churches and the state in sub-Saharan Africa.

Contrary to the assumption that modernization will invariably bring secularization, and thus a diminished role for organized religion in the public arena, recent decades have witnessed the emergence of churches as critical actors in African transitions to democracy.[5] And since Christianity is spreading rapidly in Africa, churches will continue to have a great influence on the political systems of African countries. Leading comparativists acknowledge this. Samuel P. Huntington argues: "As the numbers of Christians multiply . . . their political power will increase."[6] Michael Bratton observes that "The largest and most rapidly growing voluntary associations are the churches . . . whose ministries increasingly address secular as well as spiritual concerns, and which are federated from parish to national and international levels."[7] This work contributes to a clearer understanding of the factors that are causally linked to the episodic entrance of the churches into politics.

The book is significant in three distinct ways. First, it addresses a significant factor in African politics. In sub-Saharan Africa, Christian churches have historically been, and continue to be, the "continent's dominant religion at the level of government and of political life."[8] In 1900 only ten percent of Africa's population was Christian, but by 1990, at least fifty-seven percent of Africans were Christians. According to one estimate, by the year 2000 over sixty-one percent of Africa's population was Christian.[9] Church-state interaction will therefore remain an area of theoretical interest as well as a topic of practical value to students and practitioners of the politics of Africa.

Second, the book provides a comparative panorama. In the literature on church-state issues in Africa, relatively few studies have explored the role of the churches in a comparative perspective. Although quite impressive, most of the existing studies are single-country studies, with limited potential for generalization. The comparative perspective in this book is illuminating because it includes South Africa, which until now has been treated as unique and distinct from "black Africa." This work suggests that the factors that drew the churches into political opposition to—and eventual confrontation with—the Apartheid regime, were essentially the same as those that have led churches in the rest of Africa to actively seek political change.

Third, the work examines the role of churches as one element within the larger context of civil society.[10] Most studies of the churches are conducted by students of Christian theology who assume churches to be unique from other associations in society. "For [them] the Church is a divinely founded fellowship within which the Holy Spirit acts despite the human frailty of members of the fellowship. There is for them an unknown spiritual dimension in any equation the historian seeks to formulate."[11] Without necessarily questioning this theological position, the present work agrees with those who contend that the church "remains sociologically an association among other associations."[12] In this work, therefore the churches are examined as one of the many social organizations that exist or struggle to exist outside state control. The ability of the churches to escape state hegemony is attributed to their resources and not so much to their transcendental nature.[13]

Finally, the work introduces original information about church-state relations in cases where few or no such studies have been conducted. While South African church-state relations have received some attention in the literature, fewer studies exist for Zimbabwe. As for Zambia, this is the first major inquiry into the political role of the churches in the postcolonial period. The study also alludes, albeit briefly, to a handful of other cases on the continent.

BAYART'S MODEL

The conceptual model—model understood here as a device "used to sort out, organize, and simplify more complex processes"[14]—employed in the work is a framework of analysis developed by Jean François Bayart, a leading French Africanist.[15] Based on his observations in Cameroon in the early 1970s, Bayart published a geographically limited but conceptually powerful work on what he called the "political functions" of the churches in a nonpluralist state. In this seminal work, Bayart concluded that in nonpluralist states in Africa, "churches often replace structures distinctly political in certain of their functions."[16] Therefore, when the state suppresses political opposition groups, creating a vacuum in the system, churches assume the functions of these organizations, leading to confrontation between the state and the churches.

Bayart argued that the churches are one element of civil society that enjoys relative autonomy from the postcolonial state hegemony—they remain "zones of freedom" in an otherwise oppressive political environment.[17] According to Bayart, the churches are virtually a "state within a state."[18] While this particular claim seems a little exaggerated, it makes the point that churches in many African states effectively rival the state in the delivery of social services. Churches run hospitals, schools, colleges, and, in some cases, universities.

That some African governments are threatened by this is evident from the fact that many of them have attempted to nationalize these establishments. For example, in 1971 Mobutu Sese Seko nationalized the once prestigious Catholic University of Lovanium along with the other institutions of higher education run by the Catholic Church. According to some estimates, at that time the Catholic Church supplied sixty-eight percent of the teachers in primary schools and about forty-four percent of those in secondary schools.[19] But the fact that these institutions virtually collapsed after being nationalized illustrates the point that the African state lacks the capacity to adequately deliver public goods and needs the help of the churches and other nongovernmental agencies.

In a nonpluralist state, the state and the churches often emerge as the two powerful players with the potential for collaboration, coexistence, and rivalry. The irony is that neither can exist effectively without the other. The state needs the churches to meet its often severe shortfall in social welfare services. Moreover, the state has some interest in the socialization functions of the churches. The religious teaching of the churches (including obedience, hard work, and so on) is almost always beneficial to the status quo. The churches in many ways need the functions of the state, and this further illuminates the invariable ambiguity of church-state relations. For example, the churches need the function of law enforcement in order to fulfill their other functions. However, it is these same functions that often trigger confrontation between the churches and the state. Thus, on the one hand the churches need and want the presence of the state, but on the other hand they would like the state's role to be limited to those functions that help the churches reach their objectives.

Out of this ambiguity, Bayart developed three models of church-state relations: collaborative, complementary, and conflictual. In the collaborative model, state and church interest converge, leading to a visible "unity of action."[20] The churches and the state find that they have noncontradictory objectives in their relations with society. At best this model occurs in a political milieu where state legitimacy is high and state-society relations are positive. In such an environment, the state is eager to serve rather than to repress society. This leads to harmony in church-state relations. In Africa, complementary relations were common in the brief period after independence. In that period, the objectives of the young and promising states, often led by young and promising leaders, provided a basis for collaborative relations with the churches.

The complementary model is distinct from the collaborative model in that there is no evident "unity of purpose" between the state and the ecclesiastical bodies. The churches neither endorse nor confront the state. Neither engages in any activity that is a direct threat to the other. In

Bayart's words, the churches and the state move away from active collaboration to a cold "coexistence."[21]

Bayart uses the term "complementary" for this model because, despite the absence of collaboration and "unity of purpose," the churches continue to employ their resources to meet the state's shortfall in its service of society. Within this model we can identify the role of the churches as nongovernmental organizations (NGOs) committed to community and national development.[22] Until recently, nongovernmental organizations in Africa have tended to have little or nothing to do with the state or politics.[23] Most NGOs have focused on making good the state's shortfalls by delivering goods and services to those segments of society that, because of the state's limited resources, imbalanced distribution policies, or corruption and abuse by state officials, have benefited little from the state's delivery systems. Churches often follow this NGO model by opening schools, health centers, and other public service centers in the parts of the cities where the poor reside or in the rural areas where the state's services are mostly nonexistent. This is complementary to the state in that the public nominally expect such services to be delivered by the government and so when the churches and other civil society groups step in, the state benefits from having a relatively contented population.

However, it should not be assumed that this model is characterized by unperturbed harmony between the state and the churches. In fact it is a potentially explosive state of affairs. The potential conflict lies in the fact that it does not take long for the churches to begin to point out the link between economics and politics. It soon becomes apparent that it is the depravity of the state that is perpetrating poverty. This realization compels the churches to move away from merely complementing the state to actually questioning its policies, and by implication its legitimacy. The argument, as stated by Michael Bratton, is powerful: "Poverty is a political condition as well as an economic one . . . Poor people have little or no control over the material and institutional conditions under which they exist."[24] The complementary model therefore describes a more or less transitional state, leading invariably to conflict. The third model in Bayart's framework—the conflictual model—is of particular interest to this work because it is here that the churches are drawn directly into the political process. In this model, says Bayart, "churches compete with political structures of the regime and there is conflict."[25] The conflict is not about religion per se; nor is it about the churches' right to freedom of worship. Bayart observes that "the problem of relations between churches and the state . . . is not of a religious nature . . . incidents and tensions are always political . . . relations between [those in power] and the churches are above all political."[26]

Bayart warns that both the state and the churches are made up of a labyrinth of relationships that are not easy to decipher. "Heterogeneity of the forces facing each other, multiplicity of the structures of relations . . . dominate the relationships between the churches and the regime, and complicate the analysis of it."[27] Elsewhere he observes: "Neither the state nor the churches are monolithic" and so "relations emerge which are difficult to [analyze] in their complexity."[28]

In other words, the three models are ideal types useful for theoretical analysis. However, in reality they are not mutually exclusive. They may exist simultaneously at different levels, or in different segments of the collective Christian community. This should not be surprising. After all, civil society is, as understood in this work, "an arena where manifold social movements . . . and civic organizations from all classes . . . attempt to constitute themselves and advance their interest."[29] It is quite often in the interest of the churches to cooperate with the state in some ways and to complement the state in others, even when conflict is the overriding mode of church-state relations. For example, while the churches may be in conflict with the state over the need for democratization, they may collaborate with the state in campaigning against violence as the method to achieve this goal, and complement the state's limited medical facilities by providing medical help to both law enforcement officers and civilians who are victims of clashes between the state and its political opponents.

The power of Bayart's framework is that it delineates these ideal types, enabling the analyst to observe and explain shifts in church-state relations from collaborative to complementary to conflictual.

CHURCH-STATE CONFLICT IN AFRICA

This work advances the contention that conflict between the churches and the state in many ways reflects the state of the public arena. In an attempt to consolidate its monopoly over power, the state swells and engulfs the public arena, thereby stifling associational life. It becomes state policy to relentlessly pursue and subjugate all associations that have overt or even latent political objectives. Coercion and persuasion are employed simultaneously. At one level, state officials negotiate with the leaders of the civil society groups and promise them leadership positions in the state apparatus. At another level, police and military units are deployed to literally obliterate any potential for mass political action. The end result is a political system characterized by a domineering state on the one hand and an intimidated society on the other. A void occurs in the public arena as individuals and groups adopt apolitical attitudes (at least in public), while others go underground and adopt covert political and quite often military strategies.

However, the churches survive the state's onslaught and continue to enjoy their legal standing as a civil society group. Three explanations can be advanced for the survival of the churches. First, the churches enjoy a high level of legitimacy because African societies are extremely religious. Second, since the churches are not primarily political organizations, the state does not normally perceive of them as a threat to its monopoly over power. Thus, while the state makes every effort to either liquidate or bring under its control those groups that it perceives as a threat, the churches are not normally among them. In fact, as will be shown in this work, when the churches assume the clearly political function of being "the opposition to established power,"[30] state officials are taken aback. For example, Kenneth Kaunda of Zambia repeatedly and sometimes tearfully lamented that the churches were "preaching hatred" against his government.[31] In South Africa, Prime Minister Vorster and his minister of police reacted in a similar manner to a 1977 document that criticized the state. "Why didn't you dialogue with us first? We are brothers!" they lamented.[32] These incidents suggest that government officials do not often anticipate political opposition from the churches, and are surprised when it occurs.

Third, in Africa the churches are the one element of civil society that has the institutional and organizational structures, communications resources, leadership capability, and transnational contacts necessary to resist or even rival the state. As Bayart argued, the churches are almost "a state within a state." Therefore not only can the churches survive in "exclusion from the state" (which other groups would find very hard to do), but their exclusion often heightens what Patrick Chabal describes as the "consciousness of their externality and their opposition to the state."[33]

The presence of a political void and the churches' capacity for independent social action are the primary factors leading to church-state confrontation. The void draws the churches into the public arena and places them in confrontation with the state. The churches' own internal capacities enable the churches to engage the state. However, it must be emphasized that the external variables and the internal organizational capacities provide only the favorable environment for church-state conflict. The constituent members of the Christian community retain the volition either to engage or not to engage the state.

Thus while the repression of opposition forces within civil society is posited in this work as the explanatory variable, there are intravenous variables that, to varying extents, affect the reaction of the churches. These variables (for example, quality of leadership, organizational capacity, theological emphasis, constituency served by a particular ecclesiastical structure) are elusive and their independent effect is not clear. For example, this work shows that the emergence of the South African Council of Churches (SACC) as a major influence in South African politics in the 1980s was triggered by the void resulting from the repression of black protest movements. This coincided with the rise of the charismatic black bishop Desmond Tutu to leadership of the SACC. While the primary argument of this work is that it is the void that is causally linked to SACC-state confrontation, Tutu's background and personal traits are factors that cannot be ignored.

It is not surprising that the three models articulated by Bayart more or less coincide with the shifts in state-society relations in postcolonial Africa identified by Rainer Tetzlaff. The first phase is characterized by a "broad national consensus of the population with the government." This phase often occurs soon after a major transition such as the end of colonial rule in black Africa or the end of white rule in South Africa. It is during this phase that collaboration between church and state is most likely to occur.

The second phase is characterized by "attempts to achieve development and political progress" and by "development plans and grand projects for the country's infrastructure." This is when the churches' complementary role becomes significant. The churches often complement the state's national development programs.

In the third phase, "autocratic rule" appears and governance "degenerates into the self-defence of the state class anxious to preserve or secure its position, sinecures, and privileges."[34] The state, having lost its legitimacy, has failed in its economic policies, and, faced with growing discontent, abandons earlier attempts at popular governance and essentially becomes a police state. Police and army troops become the instrument of governance. Political dissenters are jailed and human rights abuses increase. Failed economic policies escalate the gap between the rich and the poor, leading to frequent uprisings by the urban poor. However, these sporadic protest movements are easily quelled and all other attempts at organized opposition to the state are liquidated.

For reasons already given, the churches escape the tentacles of the state, remaining, in Bayart's words, "zones of liberty" from which organized opposition to the state is mounted. Not coincidentally, therefore, in the late 1980s, when transitions to democracy swept across most of sub-Saharan Africa, church organizations and church leaders "from a variety of denominations" were at "the center of most of these transformations and upheavals."[35] It was this phenomenon that prompted this work.

ALTERNATIVE APPROACHES

Bayart's framework of analysis is utilized in the following chapters because it provides an effective model for church-state analysis in Africa. The legal-constitutional approach, which dominates analyses of American church-state issues, would not be fruitful in the African context. The boundary and free exercise of religion questions that are so potent in American politics are not meaningful issues in Africa.[36] Because African constitutions are infrequently honored, rarely, if ever, do African states and churches clash over constitutional provisions.

Another alternative is to take an ideological approach and to examine the interface of popular ideas with organized religion and the resulting impact on church-state relations. This appears to be a common approach in the work of church and state in Latin America. For example, Daniel H. Levine notes that "many good studies" have explored the "dynamic relation of religion (ideas, symbols, groups, and practices) to politics in all its many forms and levels: conservative accommodations, neighborhood movements, military authoritarianism, revolutionary organizations and liberal democracy."[37] This approach, however, has not attracted a following in Africa, in part because the impact of theology on ideology has been generally very limited. In general, church-state relations in sub-Saharan Africa do not exhibit an underlying and coherent belief system but are rather a pragmatic response to prevailing political conditions. This perhaps explains why liberation theology, as a set of ideas, did not take root in Africa.[38]

Social movement theories offer a potentially powerful approach to a study of the role of the churches in African politics. After all, African churches have quite often provided resources (facilities, leadership, and so on) and become the base for social movements—and this is not a uniquely African experience.[39] However, the limitation of this approach, at least to the present work, is that social movements are generally a terminal phenomenon while churches are relatively permanent institutions.

Others have adopted a broader philosophical debate over the role of religion in African politics. Instead of focusing exclusively on the interaction between churches and the state, they examine the interface between religion and public life. In a recent work of religion and politics in Nigeria, Simeon O. Ilesanmi summarizes three "theories" (more accurately theses) that could provide a better understanding of the "role religion should play in the ongoing search for political stability and in the overall formulation of public policy in Nigeria."[40]

Ilesanmi's first thesis is that Nigerians have failed to privatize religion and this leads to religion-driven political conflict. He criticizes this thesis for its assumption that politics can be a "neutral activity, one in which . . . beliefs about human good should not play any role" and says the argument "offends the phenomenological integrity of religion as a cultural and meaning-supplying activity."[41]

Ilesanmi's second explanation for the significant presence of religious influence in Nigerian politics is the manipulation thesis. The idea here is that political actors and other interest groups exploit religion for their own agenda. While admitting that religion has been exploited for political purposes, Ilesanmi still finds this explanation inadequate. He argues that to reduce religion to "simply a pawn," manipulated by politicians whose interests alone count, fails to appreciate the genuine religious desires to "purify" Nigeria's politics.[42]

His third explanation—the hegemonic state thesis—deserves closer attention because of its relevance to the present work. This thesis states:

The Nigerian state as embodied in the government, is its own undoing because it refuses to acknowledge its legitimate bounds. By constituting itself as the primary center of value to which loyalties must be channeled, the state has stifled the emergence of a creative and free space for mediating or buffer institutions in society.[43]

The arguments here are powerful and resonate with the arguments of this book. However Bayart's framework remains more effective as a tool for analysis because it delineates distinct ideal types of church-state relations whose occurrence is linked to the degree of the repression of civil society. Little wonder Bayart's framework has been employed in a number of analyses. For example, Richard Joseph employs this framework to examine the role of the churches in the democratization process.[44] Michael C. Schatzberg's 1988 analysis of Zairian politics distinguished three variations of church-state relations: collaboration, withdrawal, and confrontation. These variations were linked to the degree of repression of society by the state.[45] The power of Bayart's framework in helping us understand how churches in Africa are drawn into the political arena is self-evident.

NOTES

1. The term "churches" in this book refers to the general collective community of Catholics and Protestants as represented by the national bodies such as the Bishop's conferences, national councils of churches, and evangelical fellowships. Local churches will be referred to as congregations. Clusters of congregations linked to a central administration structure will be referred to as denominations. Groups outside the historic Catholic and Protestant churches will be referred to as independent churches. Indigenous churches are those that mix Christianity with traditional beliefs.

2. My conceptualization of civil society is guided by a number of authors. Marcia A. Weigle and Jim Butterfield define civil society as "The independent self organization of society, the constituent parts of which voluntarily engage in public activity to pursue individual, group, or national interests within the context of a legally defined state-society relationship" ("Civil Society in Reforming Communists: The Logic of Emergence," *Comparative Politics* 21, 3 [1992]). Others define it as "an arena where manifold social movements . . . and civic organizations from all classes . . . attempt to constitute themselves and advance their interest" (as quoted by Michael Bratton, "Beyond the State: Civil Society and Associational Life in Africa," *World Politics* 41, 3 [April 1989]: 409). For Patrick Chabal, "Civil society is . . . a vast ensemble of constantly changing groups and individuals whose only common ground is their externality and their potential opposition to the state (*Power in Africa: An Essay in Political Interpretation* [New York: St. Martin's Press, 1994], 83).

3. Although some Africanists find the concept of the state "virtually meaningless" (Chabal, 68), in this book the state is conceptualized as "the public administrative apparatus as a coherent totality" or as "the organized aggregate of relatively permanent institutions of governance" (Raymond D. Duval and John F. Freeman, "The State and Dependent Capitalism," *International Studies Quarterly* 25 [March 1981]: 106). It is "an organization within the society where it coexists and interacts with other formal and informal organizations from families to economic enterprises or religious organizations. It is however distin-

guished from a myriad of other organizations in seeking predominance over the and in aiming to institute binding rules regarding the other organizations," (Bratton, "Beyond the State," 409).

4. Anson Shupe and Jeffrey K. Hadden, "Religion and Social Change: The Critical Connection," in *The Politics of Religion and Social Change*, ed. Anson Shupe and Jeffrey K. Hadden (New York: Paragon House, 1988), vii.

5. See, for example, John Witte, Jr., ed., *Christianity and Democracy in Global Context* (Boulder, CO: Westview Press, 1993), and John W. De Gruchy, *Christianity and Democracy: A Theology for a Just World Order* (New York: Cambridge University Press, 1995).

6. Samuel P. Huntington, *The Third Wave: Democratization in the Late Twentieth Century* (Norman: University of Oklahoma Press, 1991), 281.

7. Bratton, "Beyond the State," 426.

8. Adrian Hastings, *A History of African Christianity 1950–1975* (New York: Cambridge University Press, 1979), 18.

9. Patrick Johnstone, *Operation World: The Day by Day Guide to Praying for the World* (Grand Rapids, MI: Zondervan Publishing House, 1993), 37.

10. For readings on civil society in Africa, see Bratton, "Beyond the State," 407–430, and Peter M. Lewis, "Political Transition and the Dilemma of Civil Society," *Journal of International Affairs* 46, 1 (Summer 1992), 31–54.

11. T. A. Beetham, *Christianity and the New Africa* (New York: Praeger, 1967), 24.

12. John V. Taylor and Dorothea A. Lehmann, *Christians of the Copperbelt: The Growth of the Church in Northern Rhodesia* (London: SCM Press Ltd., 1962), 121.

13. For reflections on churches as elements of civil society, see Julio de Santa Ana, "The Concept of Civil Society," and Israel Batista, "Civil Society: A Paradigm or a New Slogan," both in *The Ecumenical Review* 46, (January 1994).

14. Howard J. Wiarda, *Introduction to Comparative Politics: Concepts and Processes* (Belmont, CA: Wadsworth, 1993), 20.

15. For some illuminating comments about Bayart's stature as an Africanist, see Rene Lemarchand, "Review Essay: The Africanist as Intellectual: A Note on Jean-François Bayart," *African Studies Review* 35 (April 1992): 129–133.

16. Jean-François Bayart, "La Fonction Politique des Eglises au Cameroon," *Revue Francaise de Science Politique* 3 (June 1973): 514.

17. Ibid, 526.

18. Ibid, 529.

19. Ngindu Mushete, "Christianity and Authenticity in Zaire," in *Christianity in Independent Africa*, ed. Edward Fashole-Luke et al. (Bloomington, Indiana: Indiana University Press, 1978), 232.

20. Bayart, 514.

21. Ibid., 514.

22. Karen Jenkins, "The Christian Church as an NGO in Africa: Supporting Post-independence Era State Legitimacy or Promoting Change?" in *The Changing Politics of Non-Governmental Organizations and African States*, ed. Eve Sandberg (Westport, CT: Praeger Publishers, 1994), 83–99.

23. This changed in the 1990s. See Eve Sandberg, "The Changing Role of Non-Governmental Organizations and African States," and Michael Bratton, "Non-Governmental Organizations in Africa: Can They Influence Public Policy?" both in Eve Sandberg, *Changing Politics*, 1–58.

24. Michael Bratton, "Non-Governmental Organizations in Africa: Can They Influence Public Policy" in Eve Sandberg, *Changing Politics*, 35.

25. Bayart, 514.

26. Ibid., 516.

27. Ibid., 522.

28. Ibid., 516.

29. As quoted by Bratton, "Beyond the State," 409.

30. Bayart, 515.

31. Ives Bantugwa, "The Role of the Church in the Democratization Process in Africa: The Zambian Experience," *The Courier* 134 (July–August, 1992): 71.

32. Marjorie Hope and James Young, *The South African Churches in a Revolutionary Situation* (New York: Orbis Books, 1981), 173.

33. Chabal, 83; Bayart, 528.

34. Rainer Tetzlaff, "The Social Basis of Political Rule in Africa: Problems of Legitimacy and Prospects for Democracy," in *Democracy and the One Party State in Africa*, ed. Peter Meyns and Dani Wadada Nabudere (Hamburg, Germany: Institut fur Afrika-Kunde, 1989), 38.

35. Witte, ed., *Christianity and Democracy*, 231.

36. See Kenneth D. Wald, *Religion and Politics in the United States* (New York: St. Martin's Press, 1987), 102–138.

37. Daniel H. Levine, ed., *Religion and Political Conflict in Latin America* (Chapel Hill: University of North Carolina Press, 1986), 3.

38. For a study, see Per Frostin, *Liberation Theology in Tanzania and South Africa: A First World Interpretation* (Lund, Sweden: Lund University Press, 1988).

39. See Barbara M. Yarnold, ed. *The Role of Religious Organizations in Social Movements* (New York: Praeger, 1991).

40. Simeon O. Ilesanmi, "Recent Theories of Religion and Politics in Nigeria," *Journal of Church and State* 372, (Spring 1995): 309.

41. Ibid., 313.

42. Ibid., 321.

43. Ibid., 322.

44. Richard Joseph, "The Christian Churches and Democracy in Contempo-

rary Africa," in Witte, ed., *Christianity and Democracy in Global Context*, 233–247.

45. See, "The Insecure State: Resistance from Without—Religious Groups," in Michael G. Schatzberg, *The Dialects of Oppression in Zaire* (Bloomington: Indiana University Press, 1988), 115–133.

Chapter Two

Churches and Political Transitions in Zambia

Unlike South Africa (chapter 4) and Zimbabwe (chapter 3), whose weather and geographic location was conducive to the growth of a large white settler community, Zambia was too far to the north and too far inland to be attractive to many immigrant Europeans. Therefore Zambia has never had the kind of intensive conflict between a white minority and the indigenous population that was experienced in South Africa and Zimbabwe. Besides a few farmers along the railroad, most whites in the colony were either civil servants in the colonial government or workers in the copper mines. Because of this, Zambia gained independence from Britain in 1964 with relative ease. Zambia's independence struggle, characterized by sporadic public demonstrations in the urban areas and the brief arrest of some of the nationalist leaders, exhibited nowhere close to the amount of violence and the sacrifice that it took to finally achieve black rule in South Africa and Zimbabwe.

Soon after independence from Britain in 1964, Zambia was a relatively pluralistic society, but it eventually evolved into a virtual autocracy under one-party rule. However, mounting political discontent, fueled by biting economic conditions and the collapse of Eastern European one-party communist states, led to the rise of a popular pro-democracy movement. In November 1991 Kenneth Kaunda, the country's president since independence in 1964, was voted out of power in one of the continent's most peaceful transitions, hailed by many as a model for Africa.[1] Since then, with Frederick Chiluba as president, Zambia has been a fragile multiparty system that will be put to its first major test in the forthcoming Nov. 2001 presidential and parliamentary elections.

CHRISTIANITY IN ZAMBIA

The arrival of Christianity in Zambia dates back to the legendary 1851 search by David Livingstone for the headwaters of the Nile. Livingstone, himself a missionary, inspired more European missionaries to undertake the difficult journey to Central Africa to establish Christian mission centers. By 1924, mission centers had been established in virtually all of what was then Northern Rhodesia. These mission centers had a profound impact on Zambia's pre-independence politics.[2]

As a result of this missionary effort, at least seventy-five percent of the country's ten million people are Christian, and the churches are growing at a rate of nearly four percent per year. The Catholic Church is the largest single denomination, with 2,800 congregations including an estimated 2.6 million members and affiliates. The next largest denomination is the United Church of Zambia, with 850 congregations and over a million members and affiliates. Other large Protestant groups include the Seventh-Day Adventists (522 congregations and 340,000 members and affiliates), and the Baptist (Southern) Convention of Zambia (500 congregations and 150,000 members and affiliates). The Anglican Church, which has some historical significance, has 198 congregations, with 63,000 members and affiliates.

Besides the Catholic and the mainline Protestant churches, there are other rapidly growing church movements, particularly those of Pentecostal evangelicals. The more established denominations representing this strand of Christianity are the Pentecostal Holiness Church (261 congregations and 68,000 members and affiliates), the Apostolic Faith Mission (180 congregations and 36,000 members and affiliates), and the Pentecostal Assemblies of God (111 congregations and 35,500 members and affiliates).[3]

A number of independent evangelical Pentecostal churches have also sprung up in the cities. Since these groups are new and relatively small— and in many cases attract people who are members or affiliates of the established churches—statistical estimates are hard to come by. The evangelical Pentecostal groups, though small in number, have become significant influences in the country's politics, particularly since the rise of Frederick Chiluba to power. Though Chiluba maintains his United Church roots, in practice he is an evangelical Pentecostal and gives the leaders of these church movements greater access to the State House than Catholic and mainline Protestant leaders.

Minority religions include indigenous religious groups that are "widespread but in rapid decline."[4] In general, these groups have only nominal influence on politics because, unlike the mainline churches, they do not have adequate resources (leadership, communications, infrastructure, and so on) to engage the state. Instead of challenging the status quo, these groups tend to insulate themselves and to focus on spiritual experiences.

Another widespread group is the Watch Tower Bible and Tract Society, commonly known as Jehovah's Witnesses (some 1,800 congregations and over 250,000 members and affiliates).[5] Although Jehovah's Witnesses are generally apolitical, they have on occasion flouted the ruling party by refusing to buy party membership cards and by abstaining from voting. In the late 1960s, this led to sporadic conflicts with the ruling party. For example, in a period of six months (July 1968 to January 1969), forty-five church buildings of the society and 469 homes of the Witnesses were destroyed. However, this was the work of young party zealots and does not necessarily reflect the official position of the state.[6]

In Zambia, church-state relations revolve around the three national ecclesiastical structures: the ecumenical Christian Council of Zambia (CCZ), the conservative Evangelical Fellowship of Zambia (EFZ), and the Catholic Church's Zambia Episcopal Conference (ZEC). While these three organizations have strong theological differences, they have, as will be shown below, tended to put their differences aside when it comes to church-state issues.

This chapter examines the political role of Zambia's churches from the early colonial era to the present. The framework of analysis employed contends that church-state conflict occurs when churches assume the functions of groups and organizations that the state has either repressed or liquidated. Therefore, church-state conflict is more likely to occur when the state has stifled civil society, leaving the churches as the only major element of civil society with the capacity to engage the state. However, once civil society is activated and state hegemony curtailed, churches will generally disengage from direct political activity and to return to their more traditional spiritual and community development roles which are often welcomed by the state. Relative harmony between church and state is then restored. This was clearly the case in South Africa and Zimbabwe.

MISSIONARIES AND THE COLONIAL STATE

From the early 1900s up to 1924, Zambia, like Zimbabwe, was ruled by Cecil Rhodes's British South Africa Company (BSAC). The BSAC had little regard for African rights, and since black political resistance had been effectively crushed by the colonial authorities, there was a vacuum in the system. The missionaries, many of them serving black populations, soon found that they had to become spokespersons for the repressed African population. The missionaries "felt an obligation to speak on behalf of the unvoiced African people." Taylor explains that "since all conferences and commissions were exclusively white, the Africans, being unrepresented, were more obviously in need of some body to speak for them."[7]

Three issues brought the missionary community into direct conflict with the colonial authorities: taxation of Africans, land rights for Africans, and amalgamation with Southern Rhodesia (Zimbabwe).[8] The General Missionary Conference—an ecumenical network of mission churches active in the territory—led by Bishop Alston May of the Anglican Church's Northern Rhodesia Diocese, vigorously represented African interests on all these issues.[9]

Compulsory cash taxation of Africans was introduced in 1901 with a hut tax of three shillings. This tax was increased to five shillings in 1914, and to ten shillings in 1922. The impact of cash taxation on the black population was severe. Because Africans were not operating in a cash economy, they were forced to leave their traditional ways of life and try to find work on white-owned farms and in the emerging mining industries. Families broke up as men had to leave their villages, and in some cases travel as far as South Africa to find work.

Since Africans had no political voice or representation, the missionaries assumed this role. Bishop May of the Anglican Church was the foremost critic of the taxation system: "To tax him in order to force him to work is to exploit him for the commercial benefit of the white man. This is unjust and oppressive."[10]

In 1922, the General Missionary Conference passed a resolution declaring the tax "excessive and unjust." The missionaries went on to pressure the authorities for a tax cut. "We venture earnestly to press for a general reduction of taxation," said the statement.[11] The BSAC administrator politely acknowledged the problem, but no action was taken until 1924 when Britain assumed direct control of the colony.

The issue of land distribution and land rights for Africans took on two dimensions. The first was the legality and legitimacy of the BSAC's claim to land ownership. The second was the maneuvers by the settler community to expand their farming territory, especially into the eastern part of Zambia where tobacco and cotton farming was seen as a possibility.

Again Bishop May led the way in questioning the legality of the claims of the North Charterland Exploration Company (a subsidiary of the BSAC) to ownership of land in the Eastern Province. This is revealed in a personal letter to his sister, in which he argues that "Their title is very shady, being based on a concession given to a German named Wiese in the nineties [before white rule] by Mpezeni, the so called paramount chief [a designation created by the British] . . . who had no power to part with the native rights over land."[12]

In his official capacity, Bishop May wrote a letter to the colonial administration calling for a "fair and adequate representation of native interests"[13] when land delimitation issues were being considered. In the bishop's mind, this would be achieved only through a commission appointed by the Imperial Government. Therefore, the end of BSAC rule in 1924 and the appointment of a British governor was welcomed by the Missionary Conference.

Sir Herbert Stanley was the first British governor of Northern Rhodesia. British rule, compared with that of the BSAC, was a little more sympathetic to African concerns. Therefore, after 1925 taxes were reduced and a land commission was appointed, which eventually prevented the removal of some people from their native land.

The colonial authorities also introduced financial subsidies for mission schools and helped build an infrastructure that would make certain mission centers more accessible. For example, a grant was made to build a bridge leading to the Fiwila Mission among the Lala people in what is today the Copperbelt Province. However, this harmony did not last. First of all, in 1934 there was an abrupt ten percent reduction of state funds for missionary schools, which were major providers of African education.[14] This action reveals that the colonial government did not consider African education a high priority. Because the mission schools were basically preparation grounds for anticolonial activists, the colonial government felt that funding such establishments was counterproductive to the overall interests of the Imperial Government.

However, there is a danger in reading too much into this policy decision. Bishop May's own interpretation of the decision was that the state needed money to move the colony's capital from the border town of

Livingstone to the more centrally located city of Lusaka. "The money is wanted for the new capital!" he wrote.[15]

Nevertheless, the clash over state funding of missionary schools is less critical to this study than the Missionary Conference's reaction to rising nationalism and the reaction of the colonial government. By the mid 1930s, an urbanized black population was growing in the country's mineral-rich region now known as the Copperbelt Province. It was only a matter of time before this poorly paid and ill-treated labor force exploded. The introduction of a new tax system in 1935 ignited the first major explosion, culminating in violent strikes in the Copperbelt Province. Police killed six people and injured seventeen.[16]

The colonial government appointed a commission of enquiry composed of government officials. Arguing that what concerned natives, "concerns ourselves." Bishop May called for the creation of an impartial commission. A Missionary conference meeting held in Ndola two weeks after these riots became the forum for church-state conflict. Sir Hubert Stanley's address revealed the tension between church and state, and in some ways was a foreshadowing of the conflict that was to take place between Kaunda and the churches in the late 1980s.

"I am myself the Government," began Sir Hubert. He went on to accuse the church leaders of discrediting his government and warned them of the gravity of any further attacks on the state. His reference to threats to people and property implies that the governor was accusing the missionaries of infringing on state security. However, the Missionary Conference, according to Bishop May, was "unrepentant." The Conference president's response to the governor's speech confirms this. "We claim the right to criticize," he said.[17]

The final issue of contention between the churches and the state was the future of Northern Rhodesia. There were essentially two options. One was to join Northern Rhodesia to Southern Rhodesia to create one large Rhodesia, ruled from Salisbury. The other was to permit the small population of white settlers in Northern Rhodesia to create a responsible government like that of Southern Rhodesia. In 1938, the colonial authorities set up the Bedisloe Commission to examine these options.

The General Missionary Conference issued a memorandum in which it strongly opposed the amalgamation of what are now Zambia, Zimbabwe, and Malawi into a large empire controlled by the white immigrant population in Zimbabwe. The Conference issued a bold statement:

Our fears are intensified by the fact that the Government of Southern Rhodesia [present-day Zimbabwe] has introduced a colour bar into large fields of industry

... We definitely consider that a Government which could pass such legislation ... would be inimical to the best interest of the Natives of this country ... We submit therefore that the case for complete Amalgamation of Northern and Southern Rhodesia and Nyasaland [present-day Malawi] with control of such a vast and important unit of the British Empire by its Immigrant [that is, white] population does not commend itself to our judgment.[18]

The Conference also opposed rule by the settler community, which was comprised largely of farmers and mine and railway workers to whom, according to Bishop May. Africans were neither fellow workers nor fellow citizens nor even fellow humans.[19] Instead, the missionaries appealed for African political organizations to be allowed to exist freely. They argued that the desire for political expression and administrative power among Africans should be encouraged.[20]

While the General Missionary Conference had until then been unanimous in most of its decisions, the issue of white rule stirred dissent. Not surprisingly, the missionaries of the South African Dutch Reformed church (DRC) (which had a strong missionary presence in the Eastern Province) decided to break ranks, and in the words of Rev. J. M. Cronje stand for "principles of Guardianship ... Segregation as the soundest basis for the true development of both races." Therefore, the DRC missionaries supported the amalgamation of Southern and Northern Rhodesia precisely because it seemed this would lead to a society patterned after that of South Africa where whites ruled.

The solidarity of the General Missionary Conference in opposing the state began to decline in the 1940s. Several reasons can be advanced to explain this. One is that Bishop May died in 1940. Without his leadership the Conference was no longer as effective. However, such reasoning is questionable because quite evidently Bishop May acted with the full support of the membership of the Conference.[21]

The explanation advanced according to the framework employed in this study suggests that after the 1940s, civil society organizations that until then had been repressed and deactivated by the colonial state began to emerge.[22] The missionaries were quick to realize that the emergence of educated and urbanized Africans meant that the vacuum that had drawn the Missionary Conference to serve as a voice for African interests would soon be filled by the Africans themselves. A preamble to a 1938 memorandum to the Bedisloe Commission made reference to the reality that some urban Africans could now express themselves. The missionaries' task was reduced to representing those who were "not yet articulate."[23]

As African society recovered from the severe initial blow of colonial occupation, which had crushed any political resistance and either coopted or eliminated traditional leaders, and as the spirit of resistance began to gain momentum, particularly in the urban areas, the church leaders who had stepped in to perform the function of representing the Africans began to see their role diminish. Africans then turned to their native associations and later to the nationalist parties, for political representation.

THE RISE OF NATIVE ASSOCIATIONS

The time came in the mid 1930s and early 1940s when, thanks to missionary education and to the relative liberty of civil society during British rule, native associations began to emerge in different parts of the country. The role of mission centers in the rise of these organizations, which eventually evolved into pro-independence movements, cannot be underestimated. For example, the Livingstonia Mission of the United Free Church of Scotland established many centers, out of which emerged leaders such as Kenneth Kaunda and Simon Kapwepwe, who later led Zambia to independence.[24]

In a detailed study of the impact of the Livingstonia Mission, David Cook concludes that "this mission provided the major intellectual stimulus behind the formation of the native and welfare associations."[25] Cook shows that it was the mission centers that became the birthplace of postwar African nationalism. The creation of native associations "marked the emergence of a new social group in African society—educated men from the Christian missions: teachers, evangelists, office clerks, and storekeepers—with ideas of their own."[26]

Cook further suggests that the missionary strategy of preparing African leaders may have been effective. "By attending the mission schools and acquiring the skills which enabled them to enter the European economy at a higher level than that of casual laborer, they had become men of standing in the community."[27]

The question which then arises is why these products of a Western and religion-based educational system should quickly turn to anticolonialism. The explanation may lie in the traditional African society, which draws little distinction between the spiritual and the temporal. This worldview underlies the African church's "reluctance to divide experience into separate realms of sacred and secular, spiritual and physical, and its insistence upon an ethic that is social and utilitarian rather than individualistic and pietistic."[28] African converts to Christianity found it hard to separate religion from politics, and they were soon employing the very ideas of Christianity to question racial superiority and colonialism.

Another important factor is that the mission centers provided a place where the contradictions between Christianity and the politics of racism and colonialism could be discussed with relative freedom. As Donald Siwale, the founding president of Zambia's first native association, later put it: "We were reading our Bible and knew that every human being was the same. Our idea of equality came from the Bible."[29]

Two conclusions can be drawn about the role of the mission churches in the colonial era. The first is that in many ways they did assume the function of representing blacks on political issues. This role quite often brought them into direct conflict with the colonial state. However, these missionaries did not in general question the legitimacy of colonialism itself.

The second conclusion is that the church mission centers not only helped educate an African elite that by the mid 1940s had began to challenge the status quo, but also provided havens for the evolution of nationalist ideas. The effect of this was that the anticolonialist struggle in Zambia was clearly driven by Christian beliefs and packaged as Christian social action.

THE ROLE OF THE AFRICAN METHODIST EPISCOPAL CHURCH

The African Methodist Episcopal Church (AME), founded in the early 1800s in the U.S.A. reached Zambia in 1903. The AME's first presiding elder in the territory, Willie Mokalapa, "caused considerable concern in political and missionary circles" when he broke away from the work of the Parish Missionary Society to become leader of the black denomination.[30] The fact that the AME was an "African" denomination made the church and its African leadership attractive to the population. One witness points out that "There was great excitement about having a church which belonged to Africa. They brought cattle and other goods. The people gave gifts and made sacrifices . . . It was the people's first time to see an African minister. He was like Jesus."[31]

By the 1940s, the AME had congregations in all the major towns and was particularly active in the urban areas. It was this urban population that later provided the power base for the nationalist movements led by Kaunda and others. It was also to this population that the African Methodist Episcopal Church appealed. First, it was a black church—an idea that was appealing to many Africans. Asked why he joined the church, one of its ministers explained, "I joined because I am an African and I want to be in an African church."[32] The AME therefore provided Africans with an environment in which they could be black and still be at home in the church.

The second significance of the AME Church was that it was one place where the educated African elite (graduates of white mission centers) could interact directly with the urban poor. Therefore by the 1950s, leaders of the pro-independence movements were either leaders of the AME or frequent speakers at AME functions. For example in 1953, Harry Nkumbula, leader of the African National Congress, was a guest at an AME conference at which he said, "I feel proud to see that today we have our own house in which to worship God [built] by the black man. A man who is ashamed of his color or race is not fit to live."[33]

By the mid 1950s, the AME had become the religious haven of the nationalist movement. John Membe, the founder of the AME Church in Zambia,[34] became the officiating minister at many nationalist events. A number of the leaders of the African National Congress, including Kaunda, were lay leaders in various AME congregations.

However, the fact that the AME was an exclusively black church was a potential disadvantage in that the colonial state could have banned it with little reaction from the white-led denominations. Since even in the United States at that time blacks had little political influence, banning the AME in Zambia would have attracted little international concern. The AME church leaders therefore weighed these factors and decided to instruct Kaunda and others not to continue to use the church to preach politics. Thus by the late 1950s, the AME's political role had declined.

While the AME was intimidated by the state, and its public role reduced, the mission-backed churches, operating under the auspices of the Christian Council of Northern Rhodesia, the forerunner to the CCZ, were able to continue to provide some support to the growing nationalist movement. As Cook observes, "mission churches acting together in a Christian Council, and with powerful home churches behind them, could dare to stand . . . against a . . . ruthless government in a way which an independent church . . . that could easily be banned, could not afford."[35]

The impact of Christian mission centers and the AME has been that Zambian nationalism has been couched in Christian terms. The Christian worldview extended well into the postcolonial era. As is shown below, even at the height of his autocracy, Kaunda remained a relatively benevolent leader. This is because in many ways his politics were governed by Christian norms. It was only in the late 1980s that Kaunda began to show less and less benevolence. Nevertheless, Kaunda's willingness, albeit reluctantly, to experiment with multiparty politics and his willingness to leave without incident in 1991 reflects how deeply his missionary upbringing influenced his reaction to these events. The rise and decline of Kaunda deserves closer attention.

THE RISE OF KENNETH KAUNDA

Kenneth Kaunda was born into an African missionary family. His father, David Kaunda, was a relatively well educated Malawian minister, who was moved to northern Zambia to serve as a missionary. A preacher and a schoolteacher, David Kaunda represented the first generation of African elite members who came out of missionary educational programs, and as would be expected he was active in native associations.

Kenneth Kaunda was raised in a Christian activist home. Unlike most African children of his time, he was privileged to grow up in a home that had many books. "The most important book of all was the Bible, which the Kaunda children studied every day and in the evenings read out to the family gatherings."[36]

For this reason, it is not surprising that Kaunda grew up to be a nationalist whose convictions were founded on Christian thought. Kaunda's basic argument against colonialism was that it was immoral because it denied Africans their God-given dignity. Kaunda's political mobilization of the African population was also, at least initially, a religious campaign. Like evangelists, Kaunda and his colleagues bicycled from village to village preaching the value of personal dignity to the African people: "They tried to persuade them they were the same kind of human beings as any other. They were not concerned at this stage with the intricacies of constitutions, representation or legislation. They had first to imbue their people with the concept of universal human dignity."[37]

Like the nationalists of South Africa and Zimbabwe, Kaunda and other Zambian nationalists were using Christianity as an ideological base from which to confront political injustice. Christianity was a double-edged sword for the nationalists. On one hand, the religious basis of the message held tremendous legitimacy for Africans. It helped position the nationalists as God-sent liberators rather than power-hungry individuals seeking to usurp power for their own gain. On the other hand, since their campaign was Bible-based, it was well received by the mostly Christian white community. Some whites, for example, joined the nationalist parties because they saw them as representing a legitimate Christian cause.[38]

In 1948, the Northern Rhodesia African Congress was formed with Godwin Akabiwa Mbikusita as its first president. In 1953, North Rhodesia was forced into a three-nation Federation of Rhodesia and Nyasaland. This development further inflamed African nationalism, leading to the formation of the Zambia African National Congress (ZANC) in 1958 with Kaunda, Kapwepwe, and Harry Nkumbula as its leaders.

Kaunda and Kapwepwe, who were radical in their approach, later broke away and formed the United National Independence Party (UNIP). The African National Congress was reduced to a relatively small regional party, while the UNIP gained momentum. Britain finally relented and granted both Nyasaland (now Malawi) and Northern Rhodesia (Zambia) independence. Malawi became independent in 1963, with Kamuzu Banda as head of state. Zambia became independent in 1964, with Kaunda as president.

Two observations need to be made here. First, Kaunda and the other nationalists who led Zambia to independence were mostly devout, missionary-educated Christians who employed Christianity as an ideological tool to delegitimize colonialism. This African elite therefore went further than the missionaries of the earlier period. Not only did they challenge the injustices perpetrated by the colonial administrators, but they actually called into question the morality of British imperial power in Africa.

The second observation is that once Africans began to mobilize themselves for political action, the churches lost the unique influence they had had on the state in the prewar years. By the 1950s, as one contemporary observed, "many . . . other associations [had] emerged, to cater for the African's growing need for self-expression and a fuller participation within society as a whole."[39] In an environment of liberated and activated associational life, the churches' political influence declined from its height during the days of Bishop May and the General Missionary Conference. For example, a 1957 statement, issued by what was by then known as the Northern Rhodesia Christian Council, reflects the churches' new role as a relatively weak mediator between rival political groups: "We urge both European and African members within the Church to meet together to consider their common Christian duty in relation to the crucial political issues facing the country at this hour."[40]

Therefore, in the politics of Zambia's independence, the churches appear as a secondary rather than a critical actor. For example, in his extensive inquiry into the politics of Zambia's independence, David C. Mulford makes no mention of the Northern Rhodesia Christian Council or any other ecclesiastical bodies.[41]

That the churches had lost their unique influence is further confirmed by the wording of a statement issued by a handful of African clergy members in the late 1950s. "We are as determined as the political groups to see the end of a form of government that rules without the consent of the majority, that imprisons people without trial and has done little to remove discrimination."[42]

Obviously, the church leaders felt the need to publicly state that they were still committed to political change. Evidently, there were doubts in some circles. For example, in a speech delivered around the same time, Kaunda raised serious questions about the churches' role in society: "I do not think I have ever seriously doubted the truth of the Gospel, but I seriously question sometimes whether God is really speaking to us in the voice of the organized churches as I see them in Northern Rhodesia today."[43]

The conclusion can be drawn, therefore, that while the churches emerged as the key rival to the state in the years before African political organization came into being, the emergence of nationalist movements in the late 1940s led to a decline in direct church-state confrontation. This pattern reveals the link between the condition of civil society and the intervention of churches in politics.

CHURCH-STATE HARMONY: 1964–1974

The end of colonialism was met with euphoria in Zambia. For the first time in nearly a hundred years, Africans were free to live where they pleased, to travel as they pleased, and to be full citizens of the country. Segregated schools and hospitals were eliminated. Africans moved into areas of the towns and cities that were previously reserved for whites.

The political environment was markedly improved. People were free to form political parties and to compete for power. The government was in many ways accountable to the people. By all accounts, Zambia was a promising democracy.

The economic environment was also promising. Zambia, as one of the largest exporters of copper in the world, had a thriving economy. Kaunda took immediate steps to build roads, schools, and hospitals. In 1966, two years after independence, the University of Zambia was opened. Other

large-scale projects, such as the University Teaching Hospital, were initiated. The country was making progress.

Kaunda also made some efforts to keep many of the pre-independence
promises the nationalists had made to the people. Educational and medical institutions were either taken over or subsidized by the state and
were therefore able to offer free services to the public. Thus all Zambians, rich and poor, had access to education and healthcare. This remained the government policy until the late 1980s, when under pressure
from the International Monetary Fund and the World Bank, Kaunda was
forced to introduce fees for these services.[44]

In this environment, church-state conflict was unlikely to occur. The
only significant clash between the state and a religious movement involved the Lumpa Church.[45] This church was a cultic movement founded
in 1953 by Alice Mulenga, who claimed to have had a special religious
experience in which she went to heaven and met Jesus Christ. By the
early 1960s, the Lumpa Church had become a strong movement. Mulenga's converts refused to obey state authorities and often clashed with
members of Kaunda's UNIP. Between July and October 1964, more than
seven hundred people died in clashes between Lumpa Church members
and UNIP supporters. The state was compelled to move in with military
troops to dismantle Lumpa settlements. The movement was banned and
its founder arrested.[46]

However the Lumpa Church was an aberration. In general, the
churches were in harmony with the state. The churches continued to
administer schools, some teacher training colleges, and many rural hospitals and health centers. Church-state relations were therefore almost
entirely harmonious.

Furthermore, Kaunda's philosophy of humanism, which "tried to
marry basic ideas of Christianity and antiracism to egalitarian precepts
of nineteenth century liberalism and Fabian socialism,"[47] was welcomed
by the churches because it was not contradictory to their teaching. It
borrowed from the Bible such adages as "Do unto others as you would
have them do unto you."

The first ten years of Zambian independence were marked by relative
harmony between church and state. This again shows that the presence
of an active civil society, manifested in relative political pluralism and
an evident commitment to national development, tends to eliminate
church-state conflict. In such an environment, the churches tend to leave
political functions to those civil society groups whose mission is pri-

marily political. The churches are also eager to use their resources to meet the shortfalls of the state in its national development programs.

THE RISE OF THE ONE-PARTY STATE

On 25 February 1972, Kaunda announced that his cabinet had decided to establish a one-party state. Some background information is essential for a clear understanding of this decision.[48] At independence Zambia inherited a British-designed parliamentary system, which allowed for the existence of opposition parties. However, the only recognizable opposition party then was the African National Congress (ANC), which, though persistent, was small and in many ways regional. The UNIP had attracted the best of the country's political leaders and was also better represented in regional terms. As a party, the UNIP was so strong that its leadership was certain that before long Zambia would evolve into a virtual one-party state, while the ANC would become extinct.

Furthermore, the new UNIP government was favored by a growing economy, largely due to the high price on the international market of Zambia's key export, copper. The promising economy was politically beneficial to the UNIP government. Wages were increased and social development programs designed and implemented. Access to agricultural loans for the rural community was arranged through state-subsidized agencies. This increased the UNIP's popularity in the rural areas.

But Zambia's copper-coated economy began to show signs of rust in the late 1960s. "Economic growth disguised but did not overcome Zambia's dependence upon copper and thus, when copper prices began to fluctuate in 1969, the country's basic underdevelopment became apparent."[49] Simon Kapwepwe, then minister of finance (later to become a bitter rival to Kaunda's one-party rule) introduced some restrictions on the nation's budget. Job creation began to slow down and unemployment increased.

Before going into the details of the state's attempt to extend its control over an increasingly disgruntled population, it is necessary to examine another factor that led to the declaration of a one-party state. While the UNIP faced only nominal opposition from outside, it contained a potentially bigger internal opposition. As noted earlier, the UNIP had attracted the most radical elements in the independence struggle and thus after independence, conflict developed within the ruling party between radicals, moderates, and conservatives.

Two years after independence, Nalumino Mundia, a leading radical in the UNIP, was expelled following allegations of ministerial misconduct. In 1967, he formed an opposition party named the United Party (UP). It was banned a year later, following an outbreak of violence in the country's politically volatile Copperbelt Province.

At a 1967 UNIP national conference, regional and tribally based alliances led to the defeat of many incumbents and to the election of Simon Kapwepwe, a key rival to Kaunda, as vice president. It soon became clear that Kaunda and Kapwepwe could not work together. Kapwepwe finally resigned and formed a new opposition party called the United Progressive Party (UPP).

The UPP seriously weakened the UNIP and became a threat to the government of Kaunda. The UNIP lost some of its political talent to the UPP and there was the danger of the UNIP losing votes in the Northern Province, Kapwepwe's home, and in the Copperbelt, where the mining community has always been politically volatile. Violence frequently characterized the conflict between UPP and UNIP supporters.

For the first time, the Kaunda government adopted more coercive measures. Kaunda and Kapwepwe, once childhood friends, became bitter political opponents. Numerous UPP leaders were detained. This led to growing political bitterness among the opposition, but prevented any subsequent defections from the UNIP. In short, the UNIP was consolidating its power and silencing all opposition from within and without. As will be seen later, it was the lack of avenues for the expression of political dissent that eventually pitted the churches against the state.

The UPP was eventually banned and Kapwepwe detained. A one-party state was legislated despite the objections of the ANC, which though small had a strong following in the south where its leader, Harry Nkumbula, was based. The state's rationale for the introduction of one-party rule was well articulated by Kaunda in 1972:

The One-Party Democracy will help us to weed out political opportunists and people who have become professionals at manufacturing lies, spreading rumors, creating confusion and despondency and pretending to oppose what they inwardly welcome and exploit for their own personal benefits in the name of democracy which they have abused and desecrated. It has become fashionable in the past for any Party member . . . to threaten to quit, or indeed quit, the Party to join the opposition; for any civil servant . . . to threaten to quit . . . ; indeed for any religious leader . . . to render support to the opposition; for any businessman denied a license or loan on perfectly legal grounds to run to the opposition in the hope that if they formed the Government, he would be favored. This era in which the politics of patronage has been a feature of life is gone.[50]

The UNIP's intentions were partially honest. There were genuine threats to internal security from the then unliberated countries of Zimbabwe, Angola, Mozambique, Namibia, and South Africa. It was therefore possible that foreign forces could infiltrate a politically divided Zambia and create political instability.

The threat of destabilization, though obviously inflated by the Kaunda government, was real. Douglas C. Anglian and Timothy M. Shaw report that in 1972 one hundred Zambians were recruited and given military training in South African-controlled Namibia. Some of these people, including a former mayor of Livingstone, were eventually tried and convicted of treason.[51]

In 1975, another armed gang, led by renegade UNIP official Adamson Mushala, entered the country's North Western Province in the hope of starting a civil war among the economically deprived people of this province. Mushala was eventually killed by government troops.

This story gives some credence to the state's fear that pluralism could be used by enemy forces to destabilize Zambia. The collapse of Zambia, would have devastated the hopes of other countries in the region of gaining their independence because Zambia provided a base for the political and military operations of many of the liberation movements.

Some government actions, such as the introduction and adoption of constitutional changes that strengthened the presidency, seem to indicate that total control was the key motive of the state's actions. It may be that the state had some faith in the ability of a one-party state to allow dissent and interest representation. Kaunda, who until his last days in power prided himself on being democratic "through and through," seems to have believed genuinely that a one-party state could allow for participatory democracy. Obviously, this belief was misplaced because before too long the UNIP had became the "supreme" organization in the country and the president had accumulated powers that could be rivaled by no other.

CHURCH-STATE CLASH OVER IDEOLOGY

As the UNIP sought to consolidate its control, it was bound to clash with organized religion. The first major clash was ideological. In 1979, under the influence of the Soviet bloc, the state attempted to move away from the religious humanism of Kaunda to secular scientific socialism. The government announced its intention to introduce scientific socialism in the school curriculum. Teaching scientific socialism would have inculcated a political culture in which the supremacy of the party would have been accepted and the state monopoly of the economy given legitimacy while the influence of religion would have been eroded, giving the party greater control of society.

The churches, which until then had not reacted directly to any state policy, were shocked and alarmed. For the first time, the churches realized that the Kaunda they had initially supported as the people's "liberator" was evolving into a communist-style oppressor. In this moment of crisis, the churches ignored their doctrinal differences and formed a united front against Kaunda.

The Zambia Episcopal Conference, the Christian Council of Zambia, and the Evangelical Fellowship of Zambia issued a joint statement, which exposed and opposed the state's plans. The churches warned that the adoption of scientific socialism would threaten "the freedom enshrined in our constitution" and Zambians should "expect . . . pressure on religion and personal freedom."

The churches discerned that the UNIP was adopting socialism not necessarily because of an ideological change of heart, but as another method of control. The churches called upon their members to "take political life seriously and not to allow an oppressive system to be introduced."[52]

The government withdrew its plans; scientific socialism was never introduced in the schools. The churches had won a significant victory. Zambia was spared from the more extreme forms of socialist experiments such as those of Ethiopia, Angola, and Mozambique. The subsequent failure of Africa's socialist experiments vindicates the churches.

REPRESSION OF CIVIL SOCIETY: 1980–1989

Despite the defeat of its proposed ideology, the UNIP continued to strengthen its grip on the country. By the 1980s, it was strong enough to completely intimidate the public and any potential opposition. Those who opposed Kaunda and the one-party system were intimidated and embarrassed. Critics of Kaunda, for example, were often roughed up by members of the party's Women's League. Political dissent was considered dissidence and its proponents were subjected to harassment by the party.

Meanwhile, the president assumed unparalleled powers. He could appoint and dismiss at will government officials, civil servants, and the chief executives of the state-owned corporations. He also appointed district governors, who served as party prefects in all the districts in the country, as well as the heads of the two state-owned newspapers and the radio and television stations. Since the president could appoint and dismiss all these people at will, their primary goal became to please the president rather than to serve the public.

The party became the machinery with which to control people's lives. The party's Women's and Youth Leagues became pressure groups, forcing women and youth to join the party and to participate in the party's programs. Communities were compelled to form party branches. Everyone had to purchase party cards. Those who resisted were harassed. The party also set up what were called "Party Committees" in the workplace. Thus, those individuals who held views critical of the party could be identified. By the mid-1980s the UNIP had became a pervasive organization with total control over society. Civil society had effectively been deactivated by the hegemonic state.

On the government level, Kaunda consolidated his control over all branches of government. To run for parliamentary elections, candidates had to be approved by the party's hand-picked central committee. Critical candidates were often vetoed. The judiciary enjoyed relative autonomy, although the judges were appointed by Kaunda. Kaunda also appointed military and police chiefs. Therefore, by the mid 1980s, virtually all the political freedoms Zambians had enjoyed in the late 1960s had been taken away. The state was in total control of society.[53]

During this same period Zambia's economy went from bad to worse.[54] The colossal projects launched during the optimistic 1960s became too costly for the government to finance. Medical and educational services and institutions dropped in quality. Roads and other types of public infrastructure, which had been built soon after independence, now desperately needed repair. The government was unable to continue financing these services, and turned to the International Monetary Fund (IMF) and the World Bank for aid. The IMF and World Bank compelled Kaunda to reintroduce school and medical fees[55] and to devalue the local currency. These measures further eroded the optimism of the earlier decades and there was increased apathy toward the party. For example, the party elections in 1988—the last before Kaunda was removed—revealed serious apathy.[56]

The state also failed to balance the distribution of wealth between the urban and rural areas. The agricultural financing schemes that were de-signed to improve life in the rural areas, and had boosted the UNIP's popularity in these areas, failed largely due to poor management. The quality of living in the rural areas went from bad to worse. To maintain control in the rural areas, Kaunda coopted traditional rulers into the party by offering some of them high political positions. This later placed tra-ditional rulers in an precarious position as they were caught in the cross fire between Kaunda and the growing pro-democracy movement.[57]

However, despite Kaunda's efforts to appease the rural population, more and more people joined the urban drift. The towns and cities, which were originally designed for a small white population, could not cope with the new immigrants. Illegal makeshift townships mushroomed rap-idly in and around the towns and cities. These became the basis for an increasingly disgruntled urban population.

On the other hand, the creation of state enterprises helped some Zam-bians take up better paying positions, accumulate some wealth, and achieve a better quality of life. This group, called the *apamwamba* (those at the top), became gradually alienated from the common people and formed a class of their own. As the economic performance of the country went down, this group, despite some shrinkage in size, acquired more wealth. The gap between rich and poor widened.

It was only a matter of time before the alienated rural population and the urban poor, together with the small disgruntled middle class, would rise against Kaunda. The first eruption took place in 1986 when food riots swept through the country's urban areas. Although the rioting was triggered by an increase in maize meal prices, it was clear that the anger of the people was directed against the Kaunda government. Rioters tar-geted party and government structures. Statues of Kaunda—until then revered—were destroyed. Kaunda was clearly alarmed. He canceled the new prices and immediately nationalized the milling industry. Govern-ment troops were deployed and the uprising was crushed, but it became clear from then on that the end was near for Kaunda.[58]

CHURCH-STATE CONFRONTATION

The churches, with many of their congregations located among the poor, felt firsthand the impact of the failed economic policies. Increased rural and urban poverty was biting the population, and the clergy were direct witnesses to the erosion of hope among the people. The church leaders could also see that although many were no longer happy with the status quo, few risked challenging the state. Civil society groups had been silenced effectively by the party structure and individuals had been intimidated by state security agents. It was clear that the party structures, which in theory should have been channels for political expression, were actually instruments of control and top-down communication. It was time for church-state confrontation.

The move to confront the Kaunda government was not an easy one for the churches. As was noted earlier, Kaunda had always positioned himself as a Christian and frequently preached about the need for Christian love. Kaunda was also a frequent guest at church functions. He was also a personal friend to many of the top church leaders. Finally, Kaunda had honestly earned a father-figure image in Zambia. Thus, unlike the situation in South Africa and in Zimbabwe where the political leaders lacked legitimacy, the churches in Zambia had to contend with a president they, at least in general, loved and respected. Despite his declining popularity and some growing questions about the legitimacy of his leadership, it was not easy for the churches to come out and directly challenge Kaunda. Civility required that the president and "father of the nation" not be publicly criticized.

By the late 1980s, however, it was clear that the once-harmonious church-state relations had degenerated to virtual hostility. In February 1990, Archbishop Elias Mutale, one of the country's most respected Catholic bishops, died in a car accident. Reportedly, the accident happened shortly after he visited Kaunda. Rumors spread that the bishop had been assassinated by order of the government. The rumors claimed that Archbishop Mutale had repeatedly asked Kaunda to retire, but he had refused.

Kaunda was apparently troubled by the rumors. In August, during an official visit by Khotso Makhulu, the Botswana-based Anglican archbishop for Central Africa, Kaunda complained that some church leaders were spreading rumors that he had arranged the assassination of Bishop Mutale.[59] Kaunda's comments were disturbing to the churches, particularly the Catholic Church. The Catholic Church was perturbed by two factors: (1) Kaunda had made public comments on rumors which the Catholic Church had not officially endorsed; and (2) Kaunda was addressing a very sensitive issue with regard to the Catholic Church but he was doing so to a Protestant leader. The latter was particularly troubling to the Catholic Church because Cardinal Josef Tomko of the Vatican had been in the country and visited with Kaunda. No such comments had been made. Kaunda could also have consulted with the bishops and expressed his concern over these rumors. But the bishops first heard about Kaunda's concern on television.[60]

From then on, Kaunda and the Catholic Church were in constant conflict. In July 1990, the Catholic bishops issued a major statement in which they said that they felt "compelled to speak out on behalf of the poor in particular for the cause of justice." The statement lamented the absence of political and economic justice in the country and questioned the self-proclaimed "supremacy" of the ruling party. The bishops argued that it was the people not the party that ought to claim supremacy. This was perhaps the most confrontational criticism of the one-party state to be issued by an ecclesiastical body since 1964.[61]

The bishops' statement came when Zambia was in the middle of a multiparty debate, and its call for "justice" was tantamount to support for the pro-democracy movement. There can be little doubt that the bishops were fully aware of the implications of their statement. It became clear that Kaunda had lost the support of the Catholic bishops—the leaders of the best organized and most powerful ecclesiastical body in the country.

THE RISE OF CHILUBA AND THE MMD

Although the state had effectively silenced all political opposition, it was never able to totally deactivate the labor movement. Three factors explain the survival of the labor movement. The first is that Zambia is among Africa's most urbanized states. Thus a relatively large percentage of the population depended on paid jobs for their survival. Since the urban populations were the most politicized, it was not easy for Kaunda to totally liquidate the movement. Not surprisingly, the labor movement's power base was in the Copperbelt Province where the Mine Workers Union of Zambia, containing the movements of its most powerful members, was located. Speaking at a UNIP conference held in the Copperbelt city of Kitwe in 1987, Kaunda said the Copperbelt full was of political "malcontents" and urged UNIP members to be more vigilant.[62] It was apparent that Kaunda was refering to the labor organization whose headquarters is in Kitwe.

The second reason was inflicted on itself by the state. In its attempts to control interest representation, the state had legislated that all trade unions must become members of the Zambia Congress of Trade Unions (ZCTU). Thus the state unintentionally created a fairly powerful national structure which later on would arise and literally become an opposition party to the UNIP.

The third factor was the personal charisma and courage (some would say political recklessness) of ZCTU's leader, Frederick Chiluba. Chiluba was born in the volatile Copperbelt Province and attained a limited level of secondary education. He worked as a clerk for a sisal factory in neighboring Tanzania but later relocated to Zambia's Copperbelt Province where he took up a job with Atlas Copco, a company that supplied equipment to the mines. He rose in the trade union ranks and eventually assumed leadership of ZCTU in 1976.

As noted earlier, Zambia's economy began to decline in the 1970s, with falling copper prices and escalating oil bills. Chiluba therefore led the movement at a time when the initial postindependence euphoria had died out and Zambia's failing economy had begun to hurt the urban poor. Chiluba took advantage of this urban discontent to turn the once progovernment labor organization into a virtual opposition party. Kaunda is believed to have attempted to silence Chiluba by offering him a comfortable party position. Chiluba is believed to have turned this down.[63]

In 1981, Kaunda accused Chiluba of being used by foreign agents to incite unlawful strikes, and imprisoned the trade unionist. The courts, which still enjoyed relative autonomy (thanks in part to the vigilance of the Law Association of Zambia), embarrassed Kaunda by declaring Chiluba's detention unlawful. Chiluba was freed.

While in detention, Chiluba was visited by ministers and Christian laypeople committed to prison ministry. It was during this time that he experienced conversion. He says his conversion, or more precisely his rededication to the faith, took place as he read the Bible and Christian literature during his detention.[64] Chiluba left prison a lay preacher. The oratorical skills he had once employed against Kaunda were for a while employed in a number of churches in the Copperbelt.

The collapse of the communist states in Eastern Europe had a profound effect on Zambia, particularly since the UNIP had expressly modeled itself after some of them. Many UNIP officials had been sent to Eastern Europe for political education. Therefore, the failure of these systems, and the exposure of their corruption, caused not a little stir in Zambia. Many wondered what the future of Zambia's one-party state would be, but none could articulate this in public as well as Chiluba. Addressing the press club of the Copperbelt city of Kitwe, Chiluba advanced a simple argument: Why should Zambia maintain a one-party system after the model had been abandoned by its creators?[65] Thus the multiparty debate in Zambia began.

Meanwhile, Kaunda's popularity was declining rapidly. The economic recovery prescription required by the IMF and the World Bank hurt the masses severely. And the coercive actions of the ruling party aroused further frustration among the people. On several occasions this frustration was manifested through violent riots in which UNIP and government property were the target of looting and destruction by angry crowds. Kaunda reacted by using force to crush the uprisings.

Even some members of the armed forces appear to have been frustrated. During one incident some soldiers took over the national radio station and announced that Kaunda had been overthrown. The announcement turned out to be a hoax,[66] but it severely damaged Kaunda's standing. Particularly damaging to Kaunda's reputation was the fact that the announcement was met with singing and dancing by the public. A forlorn-looking Kaunda later addressed a small gathering in the city of Ndola, where he is believed to have been when the coup was announced. Kaunda punctuated his speech by singing "The Lord Is My Shepherd."

Following these events, Kaunda appeared to be more open to and perhaps more aware of the public's desire for change. His first step was to call for a national referendum in which the people were to decide whether they preferred a one-party or a pluralist state. A commission led by a respected judge was created. For the first time, people were free to express their opinions without intimidation. Those who wanted pluralism were free to go out and campaign; so too were the supporters of a one-party state.

It was at this stage that the Movement for Multiparty Democracy (MMD) was born. The movement's initial goal was to campaign for the reintroduction of political pluralism. The key actors in the MMD included lawyers, who argued that a one-party state denied people their legal rights; business people, who were opposed to state monopoly; labor leaders, who were natural opponents of the UNIP; and other groups that represented different interests.[67]

The churches remained outside the organized opposition movement not because they disagreed with the movement's intentions, but because they wanted to remain nonpartisan. The churches were also sensitive to the fact that some of their members were still sympathetic to Kaunda. Therefore, while clearly supporting political pluralism, the churches opted to act as agents of reconciliation between Kaunda and the Movement for Multiparty Democracy.

While the churches officially stayed out of politics, their publications (the ecumenical *National Mirror* newspaper and the Catholic *Icengelo* magazine) became critical outlets for the growing opposition. The church hierarchy distanced itself (at least in public) from the opinions expressed in its media, but said it could not interfere with the editors' decisions. This was another clear rebuff for the state. Especially alarming to the state was that the highly opinionated *Icengelo* was published in the trade language of the volatile Copperbelt Province. Furthermore, while the younger English-speaking elite was interested in political opinions, it was often unwilling to take the time to line up at polling stations. This church publication was therefore reaching and politicizing the actual voting public as it presented the opposition's message.

Nevertheless, the churches officially continued to play an "in-between" role in which they could chide extremism on both camps while making sure that change was not stalled. The Mindolo Ecumenical Center arranged for a national conference on the theme "The Zambia We Want," to which leaders of both the ruling party and opposition were invited. However, few UNIP officials were willing to debate their position publicly. The conference was dominated by the opposition groups, leading the UNIP to conclude that the Ecumenical Center had arranged an "anti UNIP" conference.[68]

Despite the official nonpartisan position of the churches, many church leaders clearly used their influence to help the MMD. Church leaders made frequent statements to the press in support of pluralism. Their main argument was that people should be free to choose and create political associations. In their speeches, some church leaders even referred to Kaunda's rule as a "one-party dictatorship" and insisted that "the hour for change" had come.

The MMD rallies attracted hundreds of thousands of people, while the UNIP's gatherings attracted comparatively few. It was clear that the referendum would favor the MMD's position. Kaunda therefore decided to use his constitutional powers to change the constitution and reintroduce multiparty politics in Zambia. "I am glad to sign this. I want to believe it is the wish of the people that we should go multiparty," said Kaunda as he gave his assent to the bill that legalized multiparty politics in Zambia.[69]

MMD chose not to disband into many small parties that could easily be defeated by the UNIP. Instead the MMD registered as one party and elected the popular trade unionist Frederick Chiluba as its presidential candidate.

The churches did not endorse any of the candidates, but pro-democracy "political sermons" became frequent in many churches. The churches helped to raise political awareness by calling for national days of prayer for Zambia and by organizing political seminars. Although the churches avoided direct statements, it was clear that most preferred Chiluba.

Chiluba responded to the churches' support by beginning his campaign rallies with prayers and Bible readings. His speeches carried many biblical references. The MMD campaign slogan, "The hour has come," had a biblical tone. Chiluba wrapped his campaign message in Christian terms as Kaunda had done thirty years earlier. It succeeded for Chiluba just as it had for Kaunda.

While Chiluba gained the support of the churches, Kaunda lost their support. His accusation that the churches were preaching hatred left many cold. Another development that further alienated Kaunda from church support was what the churches saw as his gradual drift from the orthodox faith. As far back as 1966, Kaunda had become what "the theologian might describe as a syncretist . . . he can make himself at home in a cathedral, mosque, temple, or synagogue with an ease that makes nonsense of religious divisions."[70]

By the late 1980s, many had begun to see Kaunda as leaning more toward Islam and other Eastern religions, sometimes at the taxpayer's expense. During the Gulf War, Kaunda clearly sympathized with Saddam Hussein. There were even rumors that part of Hussein's family was in Lusaka. Kaunda denied these rumors but accused the Allied Forces of "murdering" children.[71] Kaunda made a special trip to Baghdad, the objective of which was never made clear. The opposition ridiculed this as "international adventurism" while the churches took it as a sign that Kaunda was leaning toward extreme forms of Islam.[72]

CHURCHES AS AGENTS OF RECONCILIATION

However, despite their obvious bias toward change, the churches commendably maintained a nonpartisan role, emerging as critical agents of reconciliation during critical times. This status afforded the churches the opportunity to be listened to by the rival political groups. For example, in June 1991, a few months before the elections, top church leaders were invited by Kaunda to "discuss the political situation with particular emphasis on the disagreements among political parties over the proposals for a new constitution."[73] At this meeting, the church leaders first condemned the behavior of MMD supporters who had booed and embarrassed Kaunda at a recent soccer match. However, the church leaders attributed this behavior to "the suffering and hardships" of the people.[74] In other words, the church leaders were saying that this public animosity against Kaunda was more or less self-inflicted because it was linked to increased poverty during Kaunda's rule.

About the constitutional crisis—the disagreement over whether the still UNIP-dominated parliament had the legitimacy to pass an acceptable national constitution—the church leaders took what was clearly a pro-MMD position:

The national constitution belongs to the nation as a whole and cannot be considered the product or property of any one single party. We feel that the proposed constitution requires wider discussion and debate in order to build a truly national consensus. Moreover, it should be approved by a body more representative of the multi-party democracy which Zambia is now enjoying than the current National Assembly.[75]

To Kaunda and to others it seemed the churches had "put their full weight and influence behind the MMD which advocated for extensive amendments to the draft constitution."[76] While this is how it appears, an argument can be made that, at this point, this was really more than just a partisan position. It was critical that a constitution be established that would be acceptable to all. The MMD had already threatened to boycott the elections if its constitutional demands were not met. Zambia was therefore in real danger of drifting into anarchy.

In July, three months before the country's decisive election, the church leaders finally persuaded Kaunda and Chiluba to meet in a "neutral place"—an Anglican cathedral. This meeting was a result of lengthy private consultations with both Kaunda and Chiluba by church leaders. Anglican Bishop Stephen Mumba chaired the six-hour meeting, which finally resolved the constitutional disagreements between the MMD and the UNIP and paved the way to the October 1991 election which ended Kaunda's reign and ushered in Chiluba. The churches therefore played a significant role as agents of reconciliation in Zambia's fragile transition to multiparty politics.[77]

As the elections came closer, there was fear on the part of the MMD that Kaunda would rig the elections. The opposition challenged Kaunda to invite international observers, a request which Kaunda granted. Knowing that the observers could not cover the whole country, the churches created a national nonpartisan observer group, with its headquarters at the offices of the Evangelical Fellowship of Zambia. Approximately 3,500 observers were trained and placed in all the regions of the country. In the districts and towns, the clergy organized themselves into local committees and monitored the election.[78] The elections came and went with no major incidents. Chiluba received seventy-five percent of the votes while Kaunda received twenty-five percent.

Several observations can be made about the role of the churches during the pro-democracy era in Zambia. First, although the churches clearly sympathized with the pro-democracy movement, they did not assume an overt partisan position. This was because the rise of the MMD as an opposition movement had filled the vacuum that would have drawn the churches into direct confrontation with the state. When Kaunda succumbed to the pro-democracy pressure he, perhaps unintentionally, defused the potential confrontation with the churches. Once the MMD provided the necessary political representation for the opposition, the churches began to mediate the confrontation between the UNIP and the MMD.

However, it must also be observed that Chiluba's evangelicalism, while attractive to the younger generation of English-speaking urban Christians, did to some extent alienate the older generation of Christians who belonged to the more established mainline Protestant churches and the Roman Catholic Church. This conflict was contained during the pro-democracy euphoria, but erupted soon after Chiluba assumed power and surrounded himself with young evangelical preachers. When Chiluba abruptly, and apparently unilaterally, declared Zambia a "Christian nation," several church leaders distanced themselves from the statement, claiming they had not been consulted. It is ironic that Chiluba's religious fervency has quite often been met with indifference and skepticism by the major churches in the country.

CHILUBA AND THE CHURCHES

The analysis of church-state relations under Chiluba is complicated by several factors. First, Chiluba is a devout Christian who begins his day with meditation and prayer;[79] he often draws little distinction between his personal religious faith and his public role as president. Chiluba's position is that one's personal faith cannot be divorced from one's public service.

This stand often makes it difficult to know when the president is simply expressing his personal religious convictions and when he is actually articulating state policy toward religion. His abrupt, and apparently unilateral, declaration of Zambia as a "Christian nation" is one good example. Chiluba's speech begins as a prayer of personal dedication and then evolves into a presidential declaration. Having begun with "Dear God," followed by a commitment to the renunciation of evil and wrongdoing (obviously associated with the former government), the prayer then becomes an official statement directed in part to the national television audience:

On behalf of the nation I have now entered into a covenant law with the living God. And therefore I want to make the following declaration. I declare today that I submit myself as president to the lordship of Jesus Christ. I likewise submit the government and the entire nation of Zambia to the lordship of Jesus Christ. I further declare that Zambia is a Christian nation that will seek to be governed by the righteous principles of the word of God.[80]

While Chiluba's announcement was met with excitement by the small, educated, and relatively affluent English-speaking evangelical community, the reactions of Catholic and mainline Protestant leaders were cold, if not hostile. What appears to have irked these churches was not so much the statement itself, but the fact that they felt left out of the new president's inner circle. While Kaunda had worked quite closely with these bigger churches, and basically ignored the still small but rapidly expanding evangelical and Pentecostal churches, Chiluba was doing the opposite.

On the other hand, it may well be that the mainline churches, particularly the Catholic Church, whose priests are highly educated, had a broader understanding of the intricacies of church and state and genuinely questioned the wisdom of the president's statement. Such concerns were soon confirmed by the reaction of many who expressed concern that the president was imposing his personal religion on the country. Adherent of minority religions, such as Muslims, expressed concern that their religious rights were in danger. Chiluba did not withdraw the declaration, but later explained that in his view Zambia is a Christian nation with a tolerance for other religions.

In 1995, a new draft of the country's constitution brought this issue back into public debate. Chiluba, with the support of the Assemblies of God and some evangelical groups, proposed to the constitutional commission that it be stated in the preamble that Zambia is a Christian nation.

However, other churches disagreed with this position, arguing that no single religion must be raised higher than others. Eventually the Chiluba faction was victorious after a bitter and divisive debate in Parliament.

It becomes clear that, unlike Kaunda, whose ecumenism permitted him to maintain a nonthreatening relationship with all religious groups in the country, Chiluba's more outspoken evangelicalism has earned him more critics than friends in the religious community. Chiluba says he does not see himself as belonging to one religious denomination; most people seem to think he has definitely positioned himself as evangelical. This, therefore, does not sit well with other ecclesiastical groups.

The president would like to see Zambians put aside their denominational and theological divisions and join together in a common faith, but clearly he seems to underestimate the depth of theological divisions among church groups. For example, the president has invited and hosted a few American evangelists (including Pat Robertson) who are considered right-wing evangelicals by mainline churches around the world.

A more troubling factor in all this is that while Chiluba is advocating Christianity as the guiding principle of his leadership, the newspapers—making the most of their newfound press freedom—carry frequent reports of corruption and financial mismanagement in Chiluba's government. Several government ministers have either resigned or been dismissed by Chiluba amidst allegations of corruption. But critics still claim that Chiluba tolerates corruption. Chiluba pledged that he would not let power corrupt his character and that he would always take immediate steps to remove corrupt individuals from leadership positions. He also argued that corruption is a "sin problem" having to do with human nature and as long as government is made up of humans there will be corruption. Nevertheless, Chiluba claimed that the media reports about corruption in his government were exaggerated.[81] However, many people in Lusaka do not seem to understand why Chiluba retains individuals known to be corrupt, some of whom served under Kaunda and some of whom Kaunda himself arrested and charged with corruption.

Another issue that divides Chiluba and the churches is his social and economic policy. Soon after he came to power, Chiluba took severe structural adjustment measures (that would have been too costly for Kaunda to take) that left many Zambians without jobs. Large money-losing corporations, including the country's national airline, were liquidated. The government bureaucracy, which was at one time the country's largest employer, was trimmed, leaving thousands of former civil servants unemployed. Chiluba also removed food subsidies and imposed higher medical and school fees.

These measures, though arguably good for the country in the long term, have, in the short run, hurt the urban poor severely. The churches, particularly the Catholic Church, expressed concern over the impact of these measures and challenged the government to develop a safety net for the poorest of the poor. Chiluba reportedly "lashed out" at journalists for giving mass coverage to the Catholic bishops' statement.[82] But in an interview with me, Chiluba was less defensive. He argued that while his government cared about poverty, it just had no money to do anything about it. "You cannot do much to assist the poor with borrowed money."[83]

However, despite the conflicts between church and state during Chiluba's early years in power, it must be pointed out that, during this era, church-state conflict was largely focused on specific issues; there was no massive organization by the churches to confront the state. In fact, many church leaders in Lusaka believed that pointing out the problems of alleged corruption, impact of government policies on the poor, and even the bitter discourse over Chiluba's unilateral declaration of Zambia as a "Christian nation," was well motivated. The churches were trying to help affirm Chiluba's rule by pointing out issues they feared the opposition could capitalize on to undermine the young government. This was not an irrational fear. During the 1991 campaign, Kaunda and other leaders of UNIP portrayed Chiluba and other MMD leaders as power-hungry and corrupt individuals masquerading as democracy-loving patriots. Thus reports of corruption, and exponential rates of accumulation of wealth by those close to Chiluba, alarmed concerned church leaders. During that campaign, Kaunda and other UNIP leaders accused Chiluba and those around him of being soulless opportunists who cared little for the poor. The draconian austerity measures introduced by Chiluba's government— which left thousands of Zambians without jobs and in dire poverty— made some church leaders wonder whether Kaunda had been correct after all. Finally, Kaunda and his henchmen pointed out Chiluba's lack of political experience and finesse. The haphazard declaration of Zambia as a "Christian nation," and the somewhat immature handling of the debate that followed, appeared to illuminate these traits. Thus the criticism that came from the churches in the first few years of MMD's rule was really designed to spare the Chiluba government from going astray and living up to the images that had been portrayed of the opposition.

However, by 1996, when the first term of power under the multiparty constitution (for both parliament and the presidency) came to an end, it had become clear that the era of church-state harmony was ending. As the 1996 elections drew nearer, the MMD assumed, although perhaps to a less overt extent, some of the same tactics that had been used by UNIP to retain power. Political rivals and critics of those in power were intimidated and ostracized. Kaunda was barred from challenging Chiluba on the basis of some flimsy questions about his status as a citizen. The independent media, that had mushroomed during the pro-democracy era, was strangled while the ruling party retained complete control of the major newspaper and broadcast media organizations. The 1996 elections made it clear to the churches that although the civil society was still relatively free, the MMD would have little tolerance for opposition politics.

Therefore, although the MMD carried the 1996 elections, the churches were already alerted to the possibility of the MMD becoming another dominant political power in the same way that UNIP had been. This possibility became even more evident in early 2001 as the country poised for the end of Chiluba's ten-year presidency, due to end in November. Despite the commitment that Chiluba and other MMD leaders, had made—that they would not seek to extend their stay in power—a debate emerged early in the year about the possibility of changing the constitution to allow Chiluba a third term. Earlier, in 2000, Chiluba's spokesman, Richard Sakala had made several public statements in which he assured the country that Chiluba would not seek a third term. However, by early 2001, Chiluba appeared to backpedal on this commitment and the matter was tabled for discussion at MMD's party meetings. At the time of this writing, the outcome of these MMD machinations—to extend Chiluba's presidency and thus further consolidate MMD's dominance over Zambia's political life—was not clear. What was clear is that the churches which had strongly supported the rise of MMD and Chiluba as its president were again poised for a possible confrontation with the state. A number of leading clergy, and the organizations they represent, expressed strong opposition to these initiatives. Which way Zambia will go remains to be seen. However, for the purposes of this study, the Zambia experience so far illuminates the link between the expansion of the state accompanied by the liquidation of the civil society organizations that challenge it and the eruption of church-state conflict.

CONCLUSION

In many ways the political role of the churches in Zambia has conformed to the patterns delineated by the framework adopted in this book. Church-state conflict has tended to occur during periods when the state has silenced civil society. However, one major characteristic that distinguishes the experience of Zambia from that of South Africa and Zimbabwe is that in Zambia, church-state confrontation has tended to be quickly defused. This is because in Zambia, both the colonial and the postcolonial states have (in comparison to South Africa and Zimbabwe) tended to be more benevolent towards civil society. Nationalist organizations in Zambia met less resistance from the colonial state than did similar movements in the other two cases. In the postcolonial era, Kaunda's government maintained relative benevolence, thus defusing direct conflict with organized religion. In 1979, the state balked at introducing scientific socialism in the schools following an outcry from the churches. And in 1991, when a wave of democracy was sweeping across Africa, Kaunda, unlike Moi in Kenya and Banda in Malawi, who initially resisted change, was willing to subject himself to the electoral process. This defused the growing church-state conflict.

The pattern of church-state relations in Zambia, in the colonial era and in the last four decades of the twentieth century, affirms the argument that church-state conflict is more or less casually linked to the repression of civil society. When the state is more responsive to the demands of civil society, conflict with organized religion is less likely to occur. That has certainly been the case in Zambia.

NOTES

1. See Peter Burnell, "Zambia at the Crossroads," *World Affairs* (Summer 1994), 157, 1: 19–29, and Keith Panter-Brick, "Prospects for Democracy in Zambia," *Government and Opposition* 29, 2 (Spring 1994): 231–247.

2. For a study of missionary work in Zambia up to 1924, see I. Robert Rotberg, *Christian Missionaries and the Creation of Northern Rhodesia 1880–1924* (Princeton, NJ: Princeton University Press, 1965).

3. The statistics here are taken from Patrick Johnstone, *Operation World: The Day by Day Guide to Praying for the World* (Grand Rapids, MI: Zondervan Publishing House, 1993), 595. "Affiliates" are people who may be involved in the life of the congregations but have not taken out official membership. Since membership records are not always reliable, the distinction between members and affiliates may not be precise.

4. Johnstone, 595.

5. Ibid., 595.

6. Sholto Cross, "Independent Churches and Independent States: Jehovah's Witnesses in East and Central Africa," in *Christianity in Independent Africa*, ed. Edward Fashole-Luke et al. (Bloomington: Indiana University Press, 1978) 307–310.

7. John V. Taylor and Dorothea A. Lehmann, *Christians of the Copperbelt: The Growth of the Church in Northern Rhodesia* (London: SCM Press Ltd., 1962), 159.

8. Ibid., 158–163.

9. For a profile, see John Weller, "The Influence on National Affairs of Alson May, Bishop of Northern Rhodesia 1914–1940," *Themes in the Christian History of Central Africa*, ed. Terence O. Ranger and John Weller (Los Angeles: University of California Press, 1975), 195–211.

10. Weller, 199.

11. Taylor and Lehmann, 159.

12. Weller, 199.

13. Ibid., 200.

14. Ibid., 204.

15. Ibid., 204.

16. Ibid., 205.

17. Ibid., 205–206.

18. Taylor and Lehmann, 160.

19. Weller, 203.

20. Taylor and Lehmann, 159.

21. Weller, 199.

22. See "The Growth of African Self-Assertion," in Taylor and Lehmann, 121–151.

23. Weller, 206.

24. David J. Cook, "The Influence of the Livingstonia Mission upon the Formation of Welfare Association in Zambia, 1912–31," in Ranger and John Weller, 98.

25. Ibid., 99.

26. Ibid., 98.

27. Ibid., 98.

28. Taylor and Lehmann, 121.

29. Cook, 108.

30. Walston Johnson, "The Africanization of a Mission Church: The African Methodist Episcpoal Church in Zambia," in *African Christianity: Patterns of Religious Continuity*, ed. George Bond et al. (New York: Academic Press, 1979), 90.

31. Ibid., 92.

32. Cook, 287.

33. Ibid., 288.

34. For a profile, see Adrian Hastings, "John Lester Membe," in *Themes in the Christian History of Central Africa*, ed. Ranger and Weller, 175–194.

35. Cook, 289.

36. Richard Hall, *Kaunda Founder of Zambia*. (London: Longmans, 1964), 14.

37. John Hatch, *Two African Statesmen: Kaunda of Zambia and Nyerere of Tanzania* (London: Secker and Warburg, 1976), 66.

38. Colin M. Morris, *The End of the Missionary: A Short Account of the Political Consequences of a Missionary in Northern Rhodesia* (London: Cargate Press, 1962), 52.

39. Taylor and Lehmann, 121.

40. Ibid., 157.

41. David C. Mulford, *Zambia: The Politics of Independence 1957–1964* (New York: Oxford University Press, 1967).

42. Quoted in Kenneth D. Kaunda, *Zambia Shall Be Free: An Autobiography* (New York: Praeger, 1963), 145.

43. Ibid., 146.

44. Isaac Phiri, "Zambians Must Now Pay for Education and Health (London)," *Compass News Features* 14 July 1989.

45. George C. Bond, "A Prophecy That Failed: The Lumpa Church of Uyombe, Zambia," in *African Christianity*, 137–160.

46. For a complete study of this movement, see A. Roberts, "The Lumpa Church of Alice Lenshina," in I. R. Rotberg and A. Mazrui, *Protest and Power in Black Africa* (New York: Oxford University Press, 1970), 513–568.

47. Marcia M. Burdette, *Zambia: Between Two Worlds* (Boulder, CO: Westview Press, 1988), 77.

48. See Cherry Gertzel, Caolyn Baylies, and Morris Szeftel, "The Making of the One-Party State," in *The Dynamics of the One-Party State in Zambia* (Manchester, NH: Manchester University Press, 1984) 1–28.

49. Cherry Gertzel, ed., *Dynamics of the One-Party State* (Manchester, NH: Manchester University Press, 1984), 6.

50. Ibid., 17.

51. Douglas G. Anglian and Timothy M. Shaw, *Zambia's Foreign Policy: Studies in Diplomacy and Dependence* (Boulder, CO: Westview Press, 1979), 12.

52. As quoted by Arnold Temple, in "Should the Church Meddle in Politics?" *Mindolo World* 2 (1991).

53. For a good analysis of these developments, see Cherry Gertzel, "Dissent and Authority in the Zambian One-Party State 1973–80," in *Dynamics of the One-Party State* 79–115.

54. See "Economic Problems," in John M. Mwanakatwe, *End of Kaunda Era* (Lusaka: Multimedia Publications, 1994), 113–141.

55. Isaac Phiri, "Zambians Must Now Pay for Education and Health," *Compass* (14 July 1989), 1–6.

56. See Isaac Phiri, "Poll Drive a Mixed Success," *African Concord* (17 December 1987), 22.

57. See Isaac Phiri, "Zambia's Traditional Rulers Face Challenge of Democracy," *Compass News Features* (London) (16 July 1991).

58. See Isaac Phiri, "Is the End Coming for Kaunda?" *Compass News Features* (London) (11 July 1991).

59. Foreign Broadcast Information Service (14 August 1990), 23.

60. For these events, see "Dissent by Major Churches to Kaunda Growing," in *Africa Confidential* (8 February 1991), 7.

61. "Economics, Politics and Justice: Pastoral Statement of the Catholic Bishops of Zambia 1990."

62. I was present at this conference.

63. Based on interviews with an employee of the ZCTU who would rather not be named.

64. *Breaking the Chains* (West Midlands, U.K.: Christian Vision, 1992), video.

65. He repeated this argument in an address at the Mindolo Ecumenical Center where I was a staff member.

66. For the details surrounding this event, see Beatwell S. Chisala, *Coup Attempt* (Lusaka, Zambia: Printed by the Author, 1991).

67. Isaac Phiri, "Testing Time for Kaunda," *Compass News Features* (London) (15 January 1991).

68. As public relations officer of this center at this time, I was involved in the planning meetings for this conference and attended all the sessions. Only one UNIP government minister agreed to attend. He left soon after delivering his paper despite our attempt to make him stay for the open sessions.

69. Phiri, "Testing Time for Kaunda," 1.

70. Kaunda, Kenneth D., *A Humanist in Africa: Letters to Colin M. Morris from Kenneth D. Kaunda* (Nashville: Abingdon Press, 1966), 11.

71. See Foreign Broadcast Information Service (29 January, 1991), 28.

72. Isaac Phiri, "Gulf War: Kaunda's Baghdad Connection," *Compass News Features* (London) (22 February 1991).

73. Mwanakatwe, 219.

74. Ibid., 220.

75. Ibid., 220.

76. Ibid., 220.

77. Ibid., 221–222.

78. Isaac Phiri "Evangelical Wins Peaceful Election," *Christianity Today*, (December 16, 1991), 70.

79. See Isaac Phiri, "The Making of a Christian Nation: An Interview with

President Chiluba of Zambia," *Today* (South Africa) (July/August 1995), 14–16.

80. See Isaac Phiri, "Chiluba's Christian Nation" *On Being* (Australia) (8 September 1995), 20.

81. Isaac Phiri, "Evangelical President Contends with Corruption, Economy Woes," *Christianity Today* (3 April 1995), 94.

82. *News and Views: The Newsletter of the International Network of Young Journalists* (August–October 1993).

83. Phiri, "The Making of a Christian Nation," 15.

Chapter Three

Churches and Political Transitions in Zimbabwe

The people of Zimbabwe (formerly Southern Rhodesia),[1] like those elsewhere in sub-Saharan Africa, were converted to Christianity only during the twentieth century. The Christian churches, established by missionary efforts during the eighteenth and nineteenth centuries, have, over the years, played varying roles in the political development of this country. As one Zimbabwean church leader put it, "Students of comparative African politics may be surprised at the extent and depth of the Church's participation in politics in Rhodesia."[2] This chapter examines the role of the churches in the politics of Zimbabwe from 1960 to the early 1990s. In particular, it examines the causes of church-state conflict.

Bayart's observations on Cameroon discussed in the first chapter advance the contention that church-state relations in Africa vary from collaborative to confrontational. Because African churches provide various necessary social services that African states are themselves incapable of providing or unwilling to provide, their relationship with the state is often complementary. However, the thesis of this study is that churches episodically assume the functions of the opposition groups when the opposition is severely repressed by the state. In a sense, the churches fill a political vacuum created by state repression. Therefore, church-state conflict is most likely to occur when the state has repressed civil society groups and the churches emerge as the only element of civil society that can confront the state and call for change in the status quo.

To better understand Zimbabwean church-state relations since 1960, some historical perspective is necessary. This chapter divides Zimbabwean church-state relations into four epochs: (1) the colonial period (1890–1965); (2) the UDI years (1965–1977); (3) the Muzorewa years

(1977–1980), and (4) the Mugabe years (1980–1995). The chapter explores the political role of the churches during these periods and seek to link the occurrence of church-state conflict to the level of state repression of political opposition.

CHRISTIANITY IN ZIMBABWE

Because of the combined efforts of missionary zeal and colonial authority, Christianity was established in Zimbabwe in the late 1800s. Organized religion in present-day Zimbabwe is still largely embodied in the denominational structures of the missionary churches of Europe and North America.

The Roman Catholic Church, with over a million followers, is the largest group and continues to play a significant role in Zimbabwe's politics. The Anglican Church, with about 300,000 worshipers, had a special status in colonial Rhodesia as the official Church of England. This status often placed the Anglican Church in a quandary, since the white settlers in Zimbabwe formed the Anglican Church's core constituency. Blacks formed a statistical majority, but whites, for obvious reasons, were the power base of the denomination.

The third major denomination in Zimbabwe is Methodist. The two largest Methodist churches originated in the work of British and American missionaries. Today the (British) Methodist Church of Zimbabwe has 180,000 followers, while the (American) United Methodist Church has 220,000 followers. The Methodist churches led the way in educating an elite class of Africans, many of whom later became leaders of nationalist movements. For example, Abel Muzorewa, a Methodist, was the first African clergyman to be appointed a bishop in Zimbabwe. He later became a prominent figure in Zimbabwean politics.

Other significant church groups in Zimbabwe include the Salvation Army, with 210,000 followers, and the Seventh-Day Adventists, with nearly 400,000 followers. Recently, the Pentecostal movement has experienced a rapid growth in numbers. For example, the two branches of the Assemblies of God have more than 1,800 congregations and at least a million followers.[3] These evangelical movements, however, tend to be politically conservative, and are therefore less important than others for this study.[4]

Another denomination that merits some mention is the Dutch Reformed Church (DRC). In Zimbabwe, however, the DRC is relatively small and operates as an integral part of the ecumenical Zimbabwe Christian Council (ZCC).[5] The ZCC was founded as the Christian Council of Rhodesia (RCC) in 1962. It is the major ecumenical body of historic Protestant churches and some independent church movements. Therefore most church-state interaction is carried out through the Council.

The Catholic Church as a rule does not join Protestant ecumenical groups, but it holds observer status on the council. After the 1965 crisis, when Ian Smith announced the Unilateral Declaration of Independence (UDI), the churches needed a forum in which the Catholic Church would have more than just observer status. There emerged what came to be known as the Heads of Denominations—a less formal but more inclusive ecumenical network through which Rhodesian churches could put pressure on Smith's regime.[6]

Since these ecumenical networks are the focus of the political influence of the churches, this chapter pays close attention to the role of the Council and the Heads of Denominations. The actions or attitudes of a particular denomination are highlighted if and when they merit special attention. For example, the Catholic Church is quite often more radical in its reaction to state policy than the Anglican Church. Such contrasts are highlighted to illuminate specific church-state dynamics.

CHURCH AND STATE IN THE COLONIAL PERIOD: 1890–1960

Although this chapter focuses on the period after 1960, it is necessary to revisit the history of Christianity in Zimbabwe and, albeit briefly, to reexamine the role churches played in the colonial period. This provides the background needed to better understand church-state interaction in the subsequent years.

The spread of Christianity and the coming of colonialism to Zimbabwe are often assumed to have been two sides of the same coin. This is not necessarily the case. The early missionaries recognized African rule, often sought authorization to establish missions, and in turn received protection from African rulers. This distinction is well articulated by Solomon M. Nkiwane: "These early missionaries' groups could not be said to have been part of the colonial entourage. These early missionaries had come in peace, and had been granted land and protection by King Lobengula of the Ndebele. Their purpose in coming and settling in Zimbabwe was specifically to bring and spread Christianity among the African people."[7]

However, what soon became clear was that in order to accomplish their goal, which was to convert Africans to, regrettably, a Eurocentric Christianity, the missionaries needed a more dependable and sympathetic governmental structure than that provided by the traditional rulers. Therefore, by 1890 when Cecil Rhodes and two hundred white settlers occupied parts of Southern Rhodesia, missionaries were part and parcel of the colonial entourage. In the mid 1890s, when the white settlers brutally crushed the rebellion of the indigenous peoples, they did it with the apparent blessing of the missionaries. "The course and outcome of the rebellion revealed that the missionaries had betrayed their trust to the Africans."[8]

The distinction between missionary efforts and colonial occupation, which earlier on had been apparent, now became blurred. "There developed a convergence of views and purpose in the missions of the early church and the commercial colonizers in Zimbabwe."[9]

However, this convergence of interests was complex and fragile and eludes simple classification. Clearly there were missionaries who viewed their role as synonymous with serving colonial interests. This type of missionary is best exemplified by Van Buren Shumaker of the Apostolic Church Missions, who categorically stated, "We desire only . . . to aid the officials of the Anglo-Saxon governments, to control with authority the native and bid him attain to a place of usefulness as a servant people."[10]

Shumaker, however does not represent the missionary perspective in its totality. It is more or less true that most missionaries and their African converts saw "little or no connecting link between their religious concerns and the present political state or future constitutional prospects of the lands where they lived and worked." It is also true that

[a] small but influential minority of missionaries—drawn particularly from British Presbyterians, Anglicans and Methodists—went further in a political direction, who saw it as their task "to watch native interests" quite consistently, to stand up for the immediate land rights and the long-term political prospects of Africans whenever they seemed in danger either from government or settlers.[11]

From the very beginning, it was clear that the absence of an organized political voice representing Africans tended to draw mission representatives into conflict with the colonial state. For example, settler excesses in their treatment of the indigenous peoples drew criticism from mission circles. "Some of these fellows think less of shooting a Mushona than they do of shooting a dog. The burning of huts, stealing meal and raping of their women are common occurrences," complained John White, a Methodist missionary.[12]

Therefore, from the very beginning the inherent contradiction between the interests of the expanding governmental apparatus (the state) and the growing ecclesiastical structures (the churches) was apparent. The colonial state's immediate objective was to consolidate white rule. While the mission churches stood to gain from law and order and stable imperial governance, their mission (converting and "civilizing" the indigenous peoples), and the nature of the liberal Christian theology many of them espoused, invariably brought them into conflict with the state.

MISSION CHURCHES AND LAND DISTRIBUTION

Initially, a more or less collaborative relationship existed between the missions and the state. This is best exemplified by the way in which the British South African Company (BSAC) was quick to allocate to the mission churches some of the land it had seized from the Africans. Having destroyed both the Shona and Ndebele governments in the mid 1890s (apparently with the blessings of the same missionaries), the BSAC seized the territory's prime farming land and allocated it to white settlers, including the missions.

The mission churches, with apparently no soul-searching and evidently no criticism of BSAC's unjust land distribution policy, quickly accepted some of the land. For example, Jesuit priests received 12,000 acres "given" to them by the BSAC.[13] Protestant groups also acquired large portions of land. For example, the Wesleyan Methodist Missionary Society was given 9,000 acres in 1892.[14] The missionaries did not see the land granted to them as a "reward of conquest" or as "part of a process which dispossessed Africans and reduced them to [a] state of dependence."[15]

However, while the mission churches have been severely criticized for their participation in the displacing of Africans from their ancestral land, they deserve some credit for the way in which they used the acquired land. White landowners turned the Africans, whom they permitted to stay on their newly acquired land, into a landless class of near-slave laborers. To the contrary, mission settlements provided areas where Africans could at least enjoy relative liberty. For example, the 12,000 acres given to the Jesuits by the BSAC became an "ideal society in which blacks and whites were brought together in a relationship of benevolent paternalism."[16] The 9,000 acres given to the Methodists became Epworth

Mission, which later served as a breeding ground for anticolonial organizations. In the late 1940s, "the leadership which had been developed at Epworth . . . made its presence felt in certain of the associations which were formed in order to promote the interests of the African elite and also [to provide] the mouth piece for their grievances."[17]

Another significant distinction is that mission property became one place where the displaced, often poverty-stricken Africans would go for affordable, if not free, health and education services. Mission-owned land therefore not only served as a zone of relative liberty, but also as a zone of hope for the severely dehumanized and pauperized indigenous people.

Nevertheless, the paternalistic benevolence of the missionaries does not redeem them from the guilt of accepting an unjust land distribution policy. This is one reason why, when nationalist movements adopted violence as a strategy in the 1960s, some mission settlements became targets of guerilla activity. In the minds of most Africans, the fact that the missionaries used their land benevolently was not adequate to spare them from the wrath of nationalist guerillas.

The irony is that although land distribution was a powerful rhetorical tool employed by nationalist leaders during the liberation war, the Mugabe government has not been able to resolve the complex land issue. In fact, the approach taken by the Mugabe government is in many ways the same as that of the missionaries. The post-1980 Zimbabwean government has sought to redeem land from the white community by purchasing it and then making it available to poor peasant families.[18] This is arguably more or less what the missionaries attempted to do. They acquired land essentially to spare it from white settler occupation. An 1895 newspaper quoted BSAC officials as saying they would relentlessly pursue the "possession of every bit of inhabitable arable land or pasture." The missionaries hoped their acquisition of land would limit the expansion of the settler community. But this strategy did not work; the missionaries' properties were too small to "provide an adequate bulwark against such forces."[19] In the end, most of the land went to the white settlers.

The conclusion to be drawn about the position of mission churches regarding land distribution is that the missionaries collaborated with the colonial state in the acquisition of the land and the churches benefited from the displacing of Africans. The difference was that while white settler farms were places where blacks were no more than hapless farm workers, missionary settlements became havens of relative liberty for the Africans. It is apparent that rather than question the colonial state's land policy, the missionaries acquired as much land as they could and used it in a way that somewhat advanced the African cause. A striking resemblance exists between this strategy and that of the Mugabe government in the 1980s. Rather than question the moral basis of white ownership of good land, the government, like the missions, chose to acquire as much of the land as it could and then used it to help advance the cause of the displaced peasants without necessarily disturbing the white settler community. Neither the missionary strategy nor the government's policy effectively changed the status quo. Land redistribution remains a controversial issue in Zimbabwe today.

IMPACT OF MISSION EDUCATION

In their attempt to convert and "civilize" the indigenous peoples, missionary churches committed a significant portion of their resources to opening mission schools. The missionaries naively believed that providing formal education would make Africans good Christians and also mold them into subservient citizens of the territory. They saw schooling as a way to reach African hearts with the Christian gospel, as well as to make the Africans adopt European lifestyles.

Others in the white community, especially colonial state officials, rightly saw missionary schools and communities as training grounds for a new breed of Africans that would challenge white superiority. An 1895 newspaper article describes the "mission native"—one who lives on mission property and has received two or more years of mission education—as having a "gratuitous insolence acquired to perfection." Another writer in the same newspaper wished that the churches supporting the missions would realize the negative impact of conversion on African behavior: "I have often thought if the people at home only knew what sort of a creature they are persuaded into subscribing for to convert . . . and how horribly immoral, male and female, that creature becomes on being converted, those people at home would wisely keep their money in their pockets."[20]

This criticism had little, if any, impact on the education programs of the mission churches. By 1908 there were 50 schools for Africans, with 4,319 students. By 1913, there were 193 such schools, with 15,723 students. In 1918 there were 648 schools, with 41,874 students.[21] The Catholic Church clearly led the way in this endeavor. It opened a teacher training college in 1921 and by 1923 had approximately 10,000 African students and 130 trained African teachers.[22] By 1962, three years before

UDI, there were about 450,000 primary school pupils and more than 3,000 secondary students in church schools throughout the country.[23] "Considering the reluctance of the Rhodesian government to finance African education, the above figures indicate not a small contribution from the churches."[24]

The conflict over missionary education illuminates the difference between the primary interests of the colonial state and those of the mission churches. The objective of missionary programs was to create an African who had adopted the Christian religion and a European way of life. But as far as the state was concerned, such an outcome was not desirable; such an African was a potential threat to the political and economic status quo. In economic terms, such an African was not very useful to the country's emerging agricultural and mining industry. Such an African would not settle for low-paying, menial jobs on the white-owned farms or the foreign-owned mines. It is not surprising, therefore, to come across a report by the chief native affairs commissioner for the Shona-speaking part of the territory, attacking missionaries for offering Africans reading and writing skills. "It is labor we need in this country and it has yet to be proved that the educated native who can read and write turns out a good labourer." The political implications of missionary education were explained by the commissioner for the Ndebele-speaking region when he said "book" knowledge was used by Africans as a "means of defying authority."[25] These concerns were later confirmed when leading critics of the colonial system proved to be, quite often, those who had benefited from missionary educational institutions. "Without missionary schools most Africans would be illiterate, and this African [Leonard Kapungu] would not be writing this book."[26]

In 1923, a "Responsible Government," accountable to Britain, was created to replace Cecil Rhodes' BSAC, which had ruled the territory since 1890. For a while, church-state conflict over educational policies for Africans subsided. The government opened secular public schools and gave state financial grants to mission schools. Although the grants were still "pitiful" (£2,840 (sterling) for eight schools, for example), they had a significant impact. Between 1907 and 1928, the numbers of Catholic schools increased ninefold.[27]

THE FRANCHISE QUESTION

While an area of common ground developed between the state and the churches over the issue of education, church-state conflict now shifted to the question of voting rights for Africans. While the colonial state was willing to give the African population limited opportunities by subsidizing a few mission schools and hospitals and allocating them residual land "reserves," it was not about to surrender the vote to the black majority. The state's sensitivity to the franchise question was directly linked to the economic and political power of the white minority: "The European maintains his elite status by his supremacy at the polls. Consequently, few issues have as great a pocketbook appeal as those raised by enactment of a franchise law."[28]

On paper, the law did not bar Africans from voting. An order enacted in 1898 stated that all males over twenty-one who either owned property worth £75 or earned over £50 per year could register to vote. However, in practice, these requirements eliminated most of the black population. By 1910 only fifty-one blacks could meet these criteria. A Native Affairs Committee of Inquiry created in 1910 to review the franchise question not only did not question these high requirements, but concluded that blacks were unfit to vote and that their interests would be best represented by the state-appointed secretary for native affairs. Evidently, the recommendations of this committee were accepted without question by the Legislative Council. In 1914 the qualifications to vote were raised to either an income of over £100 or ownership of property worth £150. Therefore the number of blacks who could qualify to vote was still only sixty-two in 1928 and by 1938 it had declined to thirty-nine.[29]

This legislation effectively barred Africans from the political process. Their military resistance had been brutally subdued and now their civil rights were being severely curtailed. In such an environment, the churches were drawn back into the political arena and began to advocate voting rights for Africans. Church-state conflict was inevitable. By advocating African rights "missionaries came into collision with the Government."[30]

The most notable and earliest advocates of voting rights for Africans were John White, the Methodist minister quoted above, and Arthur Shearly Cripps, an Anglican.[31] The potential impact of one or two respectable clergymen, backed by their churches back home, on the small white community (thirty-three thousand by 1921) should not be underestimated. The new "Responsible" government, reported John White, "represented only one section of the Rhodesian community. The voice of the native people will never be heard,"[32] he concluded.

The colonial government's position was that African interests in the

Legislative Council would be adequately represented by a state-appointed secretary of native affairs. White, Cripps, and other missionaries argued that native councils should be established in native communities and that these councils should have the power to elect a white representative of their choice to the Legislative Council. This was a radical proposition for the time. The missionaries' argument was that the state-appointed secretary of native affairs would have little or no knowledge of African concerns. White's position was that the person who represented blacks in the Legislative Council should be one "in sympathy" with the African view of things, one to whom Africans could be open about their needs and wants, and who could speak out on their behalf.[33]

White, Cripps, and other missionaries sent letters and personal representatives to Britain and to British representatives within the colony in support of black representation in the law-making body. These activities triggered criticism from state officials who accused the missionaries of getting too involved in politics.

White's response to the criticism is interesting because it confirms the core point that churches are drawn into conflict with the state. According to White, normally the missionaries would stay away from political involvement. After all, the primary function of a mission was evangelization and the spiritual nurturing of the converts. White said that while other settlers and state officials could live in seclusion from African social and economic conditions, the clergy were "acquainted with . . . this large dumb proletariat."[34] The absence of a voice for Africans, aggravated by declining social and economic conditions, expanded the ministry of the clergy from personal evangelization to the pursuit of societal transformation. They assumed what Bayart calls "distinctly political functions."[35]

White argued that instead of political repression and economic deprivation, the churches should essentially become an opposition movement and seek to transform the status quo. The irony is that although colonial state officials criticized the clergy for getting involved in politics, the objective of the church leaders was not so much to usurp power from the government but to avert a predictable violent eruption by the repressed populace. White, for example, could foresee a time when blacks, who in the 1920s seemed to have been totally subdued, would arise and even resort to violence in order to regain their political rights. "They tell us deferentially of their desires today; tomorrow they may speak in more vehement accents and the whisper becomes a clamorous demand," he wrote in 1927.[36] This prediction came true thirty years later when the once seemingly docile black population mounted a full-fledged liberation war.

However, despite the efforts of the missionaries, little progress was made on the question of the African franchise. By 1928, only sixty-two Africans appeared on the voters' roll and this figure dropped to thirty-nine in 1938. The argument advanced by the state was that blacks lacked the formal education needed to participate in the deliberation process. In reaction to this argument, the missionaries began to see an additional role for their schools. Not only would they serve as a way of converting Africans, but it also became "their duty to train natives to qualify for the franchise and take part in the administration of the country."[37]

Meanwhile, the conflict between church and state over the franchise question continued into the 1950s. In 1941, Herbert Carter, chairman of the Wesleyan Methodist Church, argued that the only way Africans would learn about the legislative process was by getting involved. He also argued that a pool of mission-educated Africans now existed and should be granted opportunities in the political system.[38]

Church conferences became the fora for advocating black rights. Speaking at a 1943 meeting of the Wesleyan Methodist synod, Carter observed that the exclusion of Africans from the political process was "an absurdity."[39] The franchise question also drew a reaction from the Catholic Church. By the mid-1940s, the *Shield*, a Catholic monthly, in contrast to the conservative *Rhodesian Herald*, became a forum for advocating African voting rights. "Why discriminate against the African?" asked a 1946 issue. A year later, the *Shield* again attacked the franchise system. "It is unjust, and by conniving at injustice the white man cuts his own throat." In 1948, the franchise was again subjected of a scathing editorial. "Without the franchise, the African can have no real freedom."[40]

However, the state resisted changes in the franchise precisely because bringing in the black vote was tantamount to handing over power to blacks. This fear was explicitly expressed in the report of the 1956 commission set up to examine the franchise question. "It would mean that the overwhelming majority of the voters would be African," observed the commission. The commission had a problem with this because the result would be to "place the European minority entirely in the hands of the African majority." The commission would not allow this because the African majority was "uneducated and backward."[41]

It is significant to note that while the mission leaders were advocating voting rights for Africans, it was not universal suffrage they had in mind. However sympathetic the missionaries were to the African cause, they still believed that those who had not adopted European culture were culturally backward and thus not suitable to participate in a modern political system.

This attitude is revealed in some of the missionary statements of the time. In 1946, when Carter argued that the vote was an "inherent right of all the people," he also made it clear that it was the African elite he had in mind. "The franchise for civilised Africans cannot be made other than equal to that of the civilised non-Africans."[42]

The 1948 editorial in the *Shield*, which was quoted in part above, stated that "Without the franchise, the African can have no real freedom," but later made it clear that the African being referred to is the educated and "civilized" one. The *Shield* explained that "some Africans have become civilised; they compare favourably in industry, intelligence and moral qualities with . . . Europeans. It is a gross injustice to refuse these persons political privileges because the mass of them are still living well below that line."[43]

Since being educated and "civilized" meant adopting white culture, the position of the missionaries had two significant implications. The first was that Africans who maintained the traditional lifestyle lost the "inherent" right to vote; Africans had to abandon their culture for an opportunity to vote. The second implication is that the majority of blacks, who lacked a European education, would be excluded from the voters' roll.

Therefore, while mission churches should be given credit for their role during the colonial era, it should not be exaggerated. Even the most radical missionaries were an integral part of the colonial structure and mentality. While in some ways more advanced than the colonial officials, they were still operating under the colonial assumption that blacks could not govern themselves and that enforcing a European culture upon Africans was an integral part of the ministry of the church.

Therefore, the many good intentions of the missionaries during this era were circumscribed by their ethnocentrism. To begin with, they failed to recognize that the indigenous peoples had governed themselves for centuries before Europeans arrived and did not need to be "civilized." The most damaging fact is that in general the missionary churches failed to question the legitimacy of colonialism, which was one of the greatest injustices in history.

In sum, the mission churches were collaborators with the colonial authorities, while mission centers played the significant role of serving as a place where modernized political opposition to colonialism was conceived, incubated, and born. As one historian puts it, "the products of this Christian education emerged to take over the leadership of African political movements in Rhodesia."[44]

THE RISE OF AFRICAN NATIONALISM

It can be argued that African nationalism had always been present in Rhodesia. However, the brutal crushing of the Ndebele and Shona uprising in the mid 1890s and the rise of settler power dealt a severe blow to organized political resistance by Africans. It was during this period that missionaries began representing African interests. Since the ability of white missionaries to represent blacks was limited by a variety of factors, blacks made efforts to organize themselves politically outside of the state and the mission churches. Therefore, by the late 1920s a number of civil society groups had emerged. These included the Rhodesian Native Association, the Industrial and Commercial Workers Union, the Bantu Voters Association, and other smaller, issue-specific associations. But these organizations made little headway, in part because of a hostile state, in part because of poor leadership, and in part because of ethnic divisions within the African community.

In the late 1920s, Thompson Samkange, a leading black Methodist minister and a leader of the Southern Rhodesia Native Missionary Conference (SRNMC), looked forward to a time when a movement would arise that would "join together" all the native organizations. Such a movement would not "interfere, abolish or discourage the existing native societies but . . . encourage them . . . to gather and promote native opinion throughout the Colony by organizing in both European and Native areas so as to speak with one voice."[45]

The need for a national mass organization was also felt by other leaders of civil society groups. "We should have an organization that will fight for our representation in parliament," argued Aaron Jacha in a 1926 letter to Samkange.[46]

In November 1936, the inaugural meeting of what was to be the Southern Rhodesia Bantu Congress (SRBC) was held. In 1938, the SRBC formally adopted its constitution and received the immediate backing of the African clergy. Although no member of the SRNMC was able to attend to the 1938 meeting of the young SRBC, Samkange wrote to say that a commitment had already been made that "if ever an Association of the kind suggested by you is started the African Missionary Conference would give its support and cooperation."[47] It becomes clear, therefore, that from the very beginning African clergy were willing and eager to work with nationalist movements.

In 1943, Samkange was elected president of the congress. Congress members looked to this clergyman to create a national mass organization. "Most of our so-called leaders are sectional or tribal in outlook—whereas your outlook is national," wrote Brad Mnyanda, congress secretary, to Samkange, who was elected in absentia.[48]

With Samkange as its leader, the congress showed the potential to become a mass organization. In 1944, about 150 delegates attended the SRBC conference. The conference condemned the plans to amalgamate Southern Rhodesia, Northern Rhodesia (Zambia), and Nyasaland (Malawi) into one large Central African state. The conference was opposed to this idea because amalgamation was based on the Southern Rhodesian constitution, which imposed "many unfair restrictions on the African people and denie[d] them full citizenship in the land of their birth." The position marked the beginning of African nationalism and the delegates realized that this was a radical shift. "We were now dealing with real politics. We were now fighting for the country. It was no longer a question of rights, our swing was now one way."[49]

By the 1940s, the SRBC had become even more radical in its pronouncements. The influence of mission education and Christian conviction were evident in Samkange's presidential speech:

Any nation which relies upon blind force and exults in its superiority and disregards the suffering of other human races is in my mind under the condemnation of God. This is a moral universe in which God rules, the ultimate destiny of mankind is determined, not by Atom Bombs but by moral force. Racial arrogance and superiority complexes are at variance with the Christian conception of the fatherhood of God and the brotherhood of man.[50]

The fiery rhetorical activity could not cover the fact that the congress remained a weak organization at its roots. On paper it claimed to be a national organization, but it had little contact with the masses. Nationalist Maurice Nyagumbo reveals how poorly the congress had positioned itself when he says, "We heard very little about the Southern Rhodesia African National Congress and it was not clear who were its leaders."[51]

Not only was the SRBC suffering from bad publicity, it was also poorly financed. Perhaps its lack of grass roots meant that little money came from its membership. It became apparent that Samkange had not been able to convert the congress into a national mass organization. Therefore, in 1948 Samkange stepped down from leadership amidst organizational conflicts within the congress and personal controversies related to Samkange's work as a minister.[52]

The SRBC survived Samkange's resignation, but its influence as a countrywide nationalist movement remained very limited until 1957 when Joshua Nkomo, a Methodist lay preacher, founded the Rhodesian African National Congress (RANC) to take over from the SRBC. The RANC was more aggressive as it "articulated the disaffection of the black population at their almost total subjection to the small resident white community."[53] But two years later a state of emergency was declared and the RANC was banned.

However, since the law still permitted the existence of black political movements, new organizations emerged to replace those that were banned. Shortly after the RANC was banned in 1960, the National Democratic Party (NDP) was founded. The NDP was banned in September 1961, but a few days later Joshua Nkomo announced the founding of the Zimbabwean African Peoples Union (ZAPU), with himself as president. In 1963, under the leadership of Robert Mugabe, the Zimbabwe African National Union (ZANU) split from ZAPU. This split was ethnically based. While ZANU was predominantly Shona, ZAPU was predominantly Ndebele. The split weakened African opposition and by the mid 1960s witnessed violent clashes between ZANU and ZAPU supporters.

Meanwhile, black frustration was being expressed more and more in violent terms. In 1960, riots broke out in Bulawayo, and for the first time petrol bombs were used. According to a government document, by 1962 ZAPU was responsible for 33 bombings, the burning down of 18 schools and 10 churches, and at least 27 bombings of communication installations.[54] By that time the existence of an underground guerilla group had been reported. Instances of violence increased. For example, in 1964 white shoppers in a department store were attacked. The state, perhaps legitimately, was alarmed by the increased violence and banned both ZAPU and ZANU in 1964.

AMBIVALENT ROLE

The role of the churches in the politics of Zimbabwe in the late 1950s and early 1960s was, to say the least, ambivalent. The uncertainty is not hard to explain. On one hand the churches, as was shown above, had served as the breeding ground for the nationalist leaders. Virtually all the leaders of the banned groups were products of the mission churches. Nkomo, the ZAPU leader, was a Methodist lay preacher, Ndabaningi Sithole an ordained Methodist minister, Mugabe a nominal Catholic. But with some of these leaders now advocating violence as the way to achieve their political goals, the mission church leaders may have wondered whether they had indeed bred monsters.

Another factor that could explain the ambiguity of the churches during this period was that there could still have been what in hindsight is clearly a naive hope, a possibility that the racial conflict in the country could be resolved through less radical strategies than were being suggested by some of the nationalist leaders. After all, there were still some very influential whites, such as Garfield Todd, the missionary-turned-politician who had served as prime minister in the mid 1950s, who were promoting the idea of a multiracial parliament. The reason for the naivete of this hope is that by this time it should have been apparent that the white minority was determined to hold on to power. Garfield was defeated largely because he "had proved too genuinely anxious to promote African advancement for the tastes of his white electorate."[55]

Another reason for the churches' naivete was that the church leaders were still mostly white. It was only in 1965 that the United Methodist Church appointed Abel Muzorewa as the country's first black bishop, and as will be shown later, he played a significant role in the subsequent transition.

The fact that top clergymen were white provides a partial explanation for the uncertainty of the churches during this transition. While white clergy members, as was shown above, had some sympathy with black causes, they clearly were alarmed by the demands for immediate and total independence for Zimbabwe. Given a chance, they preferred a more steady transition that would have gradually integrated Africans into the political system without sudden, radical changes in the status quo. Little wonder, therefore, that the "mission churches showed themselves for the most part intensely suspicious of black political activity as being an ungrateful, dangerous and unnecessary response to the white man's tutelage."[56]

Finally, the quick shift from peaceful demands for voting rights to radical nationalism placed the churches in an unusual predicament. On the one hand was a repressive state and on the other a violent liberation movement. Adrian Hastings captures the dilemma of the churches very well when he writes that "The political stance of ecclesiastical leadership in a time of rapid governmental change is inevitably a delicate one, but perhaps still more delicate—and potentially disastrous—is its position in a period of the more or less successful repression of popular movements."[57]

This was therefore a period of rapid and in many ways unpredictable change. The role of the churches was also undergoing change. Suddenly the Africans no longer needed paternalist sympathy from the missionary clergy. Africans had chosen to determine their own destiny at all costs. The rest of Africa was also going through a period of uncertainty. Kwame Nkrumah, who was a symbol of hope for black Africa, was deposed, while trouble was brewing in Zaire and other newly independent African states. In such an environment, the ambivalence of the churches in the face of rising nationalism is understandable.

However, if the years just before the Unilateral Declaration of Independence (UDI) created ambivalence among the churches, the gaping vacuum that occurred after 1965 and the increased repression of blacks were to draw the churches back into the political arena. Nkiwane states that after 1965, "the Church had decided to align itself with the African people." The explanation he advances for this shift in church-state relations is that "it was the systematic violence mounted by the Smith government against the African population that finally forced the church to take the side of the Africans."[58] The events leading to UDI and the reactions of the churches are explored below.

THE IAN SMITH YEARS: 1960–1977

In the 1960s, the legislative body of the Responsible Government was controlled by Ian Smith's Rhodesian Front. Smith was the first prime minister to have been born in the colony, and was more concerned about the survival of the small white community in Zimbabwe than allegiance to the British monarchy.[59] Furthermore, the white settler community feared that Britain would grant Zimbabwe black rule, as had been done in virtually all British colonies in Africa. Black rule was for most whites "synonymous with corruption and civil war, arbitrary government and the denial of individual freedoms."[60]

The white settler community therefore felt threatened by the possibility of black rule. At the same time they felt betrayed by the postwar British liberalism that made Britain favor indigenous peoples' political rights over those of the British settlers in the colonies. "I have tremendous respect, admiration and loyalty to the Queen, but she is no longer the Queen we used to know," Smith once lamented.[61] The white settlers rallied around Smith's declared commitment to maintaining white rule and his articulate distrust for Britain.

The 1964 victory of the liberal Labour Party in Britain under Prime Minister Harold Wilson greatly reduced the prospects of a negotiated settlement between Britain and Smith. In 1965, the Rhodesian Front won a major victory in the May parliamentary elections, giving Smith the political support either to negotiate a constitutional arrangement that would give two hundred and twenty-four thousand whites the right to rule over four million blacks or to declare independence from Britain. In November 1965, Smith announced the Unilateral Declaration of Independence (UDI): "We have struck a blow for the preservation of justice, civilization and Christianity, and in the spirit of this belief we have this day assumed our sovereign independence."[62]

The wording of the declaration is revealing. First, it plagiarizes heavily from the American Declaration of Independence. This was not because of a lack of imagination or originality on Smith's part; it was more likely a strategic move to draw sympathy from white America, which would possibly identify with Rhodesia. Whether the strategy was effective cannot be ascertained, but what is clear is that the U.S.A. was indecisive on the Zimbabwean question until the end.

As for Britain, some suggest that Smith's announcement took the imperial power by surprise: "The British government was caught unprepared by the UDI. Despite the fact that the Rhodesian Front government had threatened UDI since 1962, the British government had doubted that people of British stock would rebel against the British Crown. The only such rebellion had been the American revolt in 1775."[63]

While the British and American reactions to UDI are intriguing, it is outside the scope of this study. What is relevant is that the impact of UDI on church-state relations in Zimbabwe is more or less as predicted by Bayart's framework. UDI ushered in a period in Zimbabwean history when the strangulation of civil society groups threatening the status quo was relentlessly pursued by the state. While, as has already been shown, the state harassed opposition organizations in the late 1950s and early 1960s, after 1965 repression of civil society reached unprecedented levels. If in the 1950s and early 1960s the state's objective was to intimidate and restrain the black political protest movements, its objective after 1965 was their total annihilation. The state put into full effect all the legislation that had been passed by the white legislature since the late

1950s. Its effect was to paralyze black individuals and organizations: a person could be imprisoned for making a statement that would "undermine the authority" of any government officer, the government was given the power to ban any organization "likely to raise disaffection among the inhabitants . . . preventive detention of up to five years was possible for anyone" concerned in any activities which in the opinion of the Governor [were] potentially dangerous to public safety or public order," police could search property without a warrant, and publications could be banned.[64]

Those who escaped the state dragnet fled into exile and regrouped in Zambia and later Mozambique. From there, they launched an externally based guerilla war. The result was a domestic vacuum in the Zimbabwean political arena. The effect of UDI and the state of emergency "formally eliminated the possibility of a significant internal African political presence . . . Protest inside the country against the Smith regime was impossible."[65]

Did this vacuum, as this study proposes, prompt greater political activity by the churches? This clearly was the case in Zimbabwe. With ZAPU and ZANU forced into exile and a growing number of black civic leaders either in jail or in exile, the churches were the only civil society group that had the leadership and organizational capacity to challenge the state. The churches provided respected black leaders, publications, and church gatherings at which state policies could be questioned. The state could not ban the churches as it had other civil society organizations for two reasons: (1) The state derived its own legitimacy from its claims to being Christian and could not afford to jeopardize this position; (2) The churches were major partners with the state in the provision of critical social services such as education, hospitals, and other community services. The state could not easily dispense with this relationship. The churches, therefore, emerged as the only legally constituted group in society that could enter the public arena and publicly challenge the state. "The banning of African political parties and the *African Daily News* . . . left a void which [churches] sought to fill."[66]

Anglican Ambivalence

Because the churches were not monolithic, their response to UDI varied. Of all the major denominations in the country, the Anglican Church was in the most delicate position. There were three key reasons for this. First, the Anglican Church, as an offshoot of the official Church of England (the bishops in the colonies were appointed by the British prime minister), had close ties to the British government against which Smith had rebelled. Second, the Anglican Church was the home church of most of the English immigrants who had made Zimbabwe their home, and many of them were either supportive of or at least sympathetic to Smith. Third, the Anglican clergy was mostly composed of white Englishmen with families, who (in contrast to the Catholic Church's celibate clergy) had "become part and parcel with white society."[67]

These factors help explain Anglican ambivalence during the UDI years. The immediate reaction of some Anglican Church leaders was to declare Smith's act illegal. "I repudiate this illegal act," Anglican Bishop Alderson said. In 1966, the Anglican church rebuffed Smith by refusing to participate in the celebration marking the first anniversary of UDI. "As I see it, [UDI] was [not] prompted by Christian ideals," said Dean Wood of the Salisbury Cathedral.[68]

However, over time some of the top clergymen in the Anglican Church became less critical of the legitimacy of the state. In part, this was because the church was not willing to antagonize its white membership, which provided its financial support. The reality, as Wood later observed, was that when a priest championed the African cause, he was likely to antagonize Europeans who, in fact, "hold the purse."[69]

Another factor that caused the Anglican Church to soften its criticism of Ian Smith was the escalating guerrilla war.[70] The Anglican Church's white constituency was terrified of "communist terrorists" and saw Smith's efforts to build a strong Rhodesia as justified under those circumstances. In 1976 Bishop Burrough was reported to have considered making a pastoral visit to Manicaland in a military vehicle, although junior priests felt it would be inappropriate for the bishop to be seen with the army.[71] The Anglican hierarchy seems to have felt that the Rhodesian army was fighting for a legitimate cause and, by implication, that the use of force by the nationalist movements to advance their political cause was morally unjustifiable and was actually criminal. The fact that Bishop Burrough later referred to the ZAPU and ZANU forces as "armed marauders" demonstrates his bias.

The excesses of the guerilla war seemed to affirm the view that the guerrillas were criminals. In 1978, the nationalist guerrillas shot down a civilian airplane and allegedly killed all the white survivors. A top Anglican clergyman condemned the nationalists as Marxists to whom "human life is cheap."[72]

Ironically, the same could have been said of Smith's regime. Human lives were expendable for the sake of the well-being of the white supremacist state. Many lives were also lost in Zambia and other frontline states as the Rhodesian air force raided refugee camps in these countries. The top Anglican leaders remained silent about this type of violence, but did not hesitate to criticize the violence organized by nationalists.

However, there is a qualitative difference between the Anglican Church's ties to the Rhodesian government and Rhodesia and the DRC's ties to the apartheid government of South Africa. The Anglican Church did not provide a theological basis for its position. Most of its reactions were pragmatic responses to an unpredictable political situation.

It should also be noted that unlike the Catholic Church, whose official stand on issues is often summed up in bishops' statements, Anglican bishops operate independently. Thus, what one individual bishop says does not necessarily reflect the position of the whole group. For example, it is quite evident that Bishop Burrough was more supportive of Smith, while Bishop Skelton of Matebeleland was more understanding of the nationalist cause. However, the influence of the bishops' political positions on church-state relations should not be underestimated. For example, after the pro-nationalist Bishop Skelton left the country in 1970, the Anglican Church gradually adopted a more pro-white position, taking up individual injustices but not questioning the basic constitutionality of Smith's regime.[73]

With the pro-nationalist Bishop Skelton out of the country and the guerilla war escalating, the Anglican hierarchy began to favor an internally negotiated settlement. Taking their attitude in good faith, it would seem that the Anglican hierarchy did not necessarily support white dominion, but was simply opposed to the excesses of guerilla war and felt that a peaceful, internally negotiated process would be better for the country. What the hierarchy failed to appreciate was that the exiled nationalist movements had resorted to the use of violence only after all peaceful methods had failed.

Ecumenical Response

The Anglican Church leaders' ambivalent reaction to the void that opened up in the political system after 1965 was singled out for analysis above precisely because it was an aberration and does not represent the reaction of the collective community of the Protestants and Catholics. In general, the churches reacted to the void by more or less assuming the functions of the civil society groups that had been deactivated by the policies of the state. Hastings observes that while the "official Anglican Church . . . moved steadily nearer the settler position during these years," the other major churches (particularly Catholics and Methodists) "moved almost equally steadily towards a public championing of African interests."[74]

Therefore, during the UDI years the ecumenical Rhodesian Christian Council (dominated by Methodists) and the Catholic Church emerged as a significant influence in the politics of the country. The void provided the churches with an opportunity to exert a significant influence in politics and for church leaders to do double duty as both clergy and political leaders. This explains the rise of Bishop Muzorewa as a key actor in the politics of this era.

The churches (defined as the collective community of Protestant churches and the Catholic Church) entered the political arena primarily through the Rhodesian Christian Council (RCC). The RCC, an ecumenical network of major Protestant churches created in 1962 out of the Southern Rhodesia Christian Conference, became involved in politics early in its life. At its first meeting in November 1964, at a time when the white minority led by Ian Smith was pushing for immediate independence, the RCC said it was "gravely disturbed" by this white initiative and predicted that it would lead to "increased bitterness."[75]

Thus by 1965, when Smith announced UDI, the RCC was already poised to assume a political role and immediately declared Smith's action an "unlawful act." The RCC went on to express its concerns about human rights and the stifling of civil society by the state: "We note the intimidation of both black and white is increasing. . . . As a result, more people than ever are now afraid to exercise their right of freedom of speech . . . people are taken away from their homes [and] it is an offence for friends or relatives to make known their whereabouts."[76]

This statement reveals some key characteristics of the RCC's approach to the political issues of the time. First, the RCC avoided taking sides in the conflict. The reference to the "intimidation of both black and white" is an attempt to criticize the use of force and intimidation both by the state security forces and by the armed units of the liberation organizations.

Second, the churches addressed the issue of free speech. In other words, the church leaders were making it clear that they had been compelled to intervene in national politics in part because of a void created by the repression of free speech. The link between the absence of free speech, that is, of an active associational life, and the political role of the churches conforms to the thesis of this study.

Third, the church leaders said the issue of human rights abuse was "serious" and had in part compelled them to directly confront the state. The conflict over human rights was later linked to the debate over the death sentence. As the guerilla war escalated, the state became more repressive and quick to invoke the death sentence as a way of intimidating the black population. The state wanted political prisoners killed, but the churches argued that systemic injustice was to blame for the escalation of political crimes, and therefore the use of the death penalty in these cases was immoral.

It could be inferred that the churches were in effect questioning the legitimacy of the state and by implication its right to administer law and order and its ability to deliver justice. A 1968 statement issued by the RCC makes it apparent that, in general, the churches believed that many of the people on Rhodesia's death row for political reasons had been compelled to break the law because of societal injustice. The statement asserts that many of the people "in our goals today, including those condemned to death . . . in normal times would probably have lived their lives without breaking the law."[77]

Along with the above issues, the churches also confronted and opposed the move by the state to adopt South African-style apartheid. The white minority in Zimbabwe, impressed by the seeming success of apartheid in neighboring South Africa, took steps to adopt apartheid as the official policy of Zimbabwe. When the shift became apparent "the church, by and large, chose to identify with the African people."[78] In 1967, the RCC published a statement expressing deep concern that the government was discussing a policy of apartheid for Rhodesia and calling upon its members "to recognize the dangers that threaten the peace, welfare and progress of our country from the promotion of racial division amongst our people."[79]

Catholic Response

The Catholic Church was not a member of the RCC, but held observer status and approved of the RCC's criticism of the state's behavior. In comparison with the Anglican Church, which tended to be a church of the establishment, the Catholic Church was less attached to the status quo and therefore found it less difficult to confront the state. Furthermore, the Catholic Church was not only the country's largest single denomination, it also controlled schools, hospitals, and printing presses and this positioned it as a potential rival of the state. Hastings provides insight into the combination of factors that enhanced the Catholic Church's position as a critic of the state: "With far more considerable resources than any other church and less dependent on white society, they . . . stuck to their guns as the most forceful independent critics of government . . . Their clergy, predominantly foreign and wholly unmarried, tended to be far less identified with the settler population."[80]

The role and impact of the Catholic Church in Zimbabwe's politics is extensive and can only be summarized in this chapter.[81] In 1959, the Catholic Church issued a pastoral letter that set the tone of the church's political role in the 1960s (Bishop Donald Lamont of Umtali led this effort and was later arrested and expelled from the country). In *A Purchased People*, the bishops stated that Africans were, like everybody else, beneficiaries of the redemptive ministry of Christ which made them equal to whites.[82] By 1965 the Catholic Church had become increasingly vocal and was clearly opposed to the Smith regime.[83]

The reaction of the Catholic Church to UDI was therefore predictable. UDI was announced while the Catholic bishops were in Rome attending Vatican Council meetings. The Vatican immediately declared the Zimbabwe situation "grave" and asked the bishops from that country to cut short their stay in Rome. The highest-ranking Catholic official in Zimbabwe, Vicar General Father Geoghegan, issued a statement saying a declaration of independence, "as a means to secure a state of affairs which will be unjust to a section of the community, would be wrong."[84]

The Catholic Church also condemned the government's use of emergency powers to censor the press. An editorial in the Catholic newspaper *Moto* read: "It [UDI] is indeed a blow not for preservation of justice, civilization and Christianity, but against it." When the column was censored, the newspaper decided to run with a blank editorial column. Upon their return, the bishops released *A Plea for Peace*, in which they unanimously challenged UDI: "vast numbers of the people of Rhodesia are bitterly opposed to the unilateral declaration of independence . . . It is simply . . . untrue that the masses . . . have consented by their silence. Their silence is the silence of fear, of disappointment, of hopelessness. It is a dangerous silence."[85]

Using its emergency powers, the government forced the bishops to submit the galley proofs of their statement for censorship. The government then directed that the above-quoted portion of the statement be deleted from the local-language editions of the statement. Later, even the English edition was seized by police during a service, and the director of Mambo Press, the Catholic publishing house that produced the statement, was charged under the State of Emergency Act. The charges were dropped two weeks later.[86] The fact that the charges were dropped confirms that the state is often reluctant to appear to be persecuting the churches. This is why churches can get away with political opposition while other civil society groups are stifled.

The Catholic Church was also relentless in its criticism of a variety of state policies and their impact on the African majority. During the UDI years, the Catholic Church became a vocal public critic of the state's racial and economic injustices. According to one Catholic bishop's statement, "Look at the inequitable distribution of land in this country; the scandal of those working conditions in which normal family life is made impossible; the often inadequate wages paid to servants, the humiliation of discriminatory legislation, the inequalities of opportunity in education. Examine these things and judge if we can ever be a united and happy people while they remain."[87]

In 1975, the Catholic Church produced *The Man in The Middle*, documenting human rights abuses by the government troops who were pursuing the guerrillas.[88] Since the government was trying to suppress these allegations, the document embarrassed the state and helped the cause of the liberation movements.

Joint Effort between Catholics and Protestants

Faced with growing hostility from the state and the increased number of issues on which the state and the church differed, it became necessary for the churches to form an alliance that would remove the "Protestant" and "Catholic" labels and give the churches one voice. The alliance that emerged was called the Heads of Denominations—a forum and network open to all heads of denominations. The alliance was more effective in some ways than the RCC because it served as a voluntary association of top clergy members, and therefore it was more inclusive and possibly more responsive to the general issues affecting the churches.

In 1969, land distribution became an issue of contention between the churches and the state. The white Rhodesian parliament passed the Land Tenure Act, which demarcated land into "European" and "African" portions. The minority white settler community received 44,952,900 acres, while the much larger African community was given 44,944,500 acres.[89]

The Catholic Church, with its large mission properties, led the attack against this act: "It may be that we shall also be denied . . . the right to educate in our schools whomsoever we will . . . be forced to refuse hospital beds to anyone not of the race approved . . . Priests and nuns and teaching brothers may have to be segregated in their communities according to their racial origins."[90]

This time the bishops threatened action. If the government would not revise the act, they would close the schools. Smith's government did not revise the act, but instead declared that the churches would not be affected by it. Although the churches were not able to stop the legislation that denied Africans most of the country's fertile land, they still registered their displeasure with the act at a time when there was virtually no political opposition within the country.

The continuing contentiousness of land distribution is revealed in a 1971 RCC statement that criticized the state's land policy for having given inadequate attention to the African cultural need to call a piece of ancestral land their home. The churches also warned the state that they would "not stand silent when injustice is being done."[91]

THE RISE OF BISHOP MUZOREWA: 1971–1979

From 1971 to 1979, church-state conflict in Zimbabwe became, for better or for worse, intertwined with the life and work of Bishop Abel Muzorewa of the United Methodist Church. Muzorewa was born in 1925 of first-generation Methodist parents, and became a beneficiary of missionary education. Muzorewa went to a prestigious missionary-run boarding school known as Old Umtali, not by choice, but because his parents had no option. In the 1930s, schools for Africans were church-run.[92] Muzorewa supports the point made earlier in this chapter that missionary education had a great impact on the generation of Africans that emerged to lead the liberation struggle and later the new government: "Zimbabwe owes a debt of gratitude to those missionaries and other church leaders who pioneered African education in our country. Until recently most educated Zimbabweans received all their schooling and scholarships for advanced studies through the church."[93]

Muzorewa epitomizes this indebtedness to missionary benevolence. In 1958 he arrived in Columbia, Missouri, to study at a Methodist institution. His five-year stay in the U.S.A. happened to coincide with the period in American history when racial conflict was high. Martin Luther

King Jr.'s Christian activism had an obvious impact on him. "He [King] always spoke without hate," Muzorewa later observed.[94]

After graduate education, Muzorewa returned to Zimbabwe in 1963. His five-year absence, and the impact of the civil rights movement in the U.S.A., afforded him a penetrating view of his country's political problems. "My people were . . . oppressed and depressed." He was also able to see the latent ethnic conflict in the nationalist organizations. "They were without a united spirit."[95] Ironically, this deep desire to build a united front may eventually have led to his isolation in Zimbabwean politics.

Muzorewa's return was timely. In the mid 1960s the churches had a unique opportunity to influence the politics of the country because all African nationalist organizations had been banned. Muzorewa was instrumental in the creation of the RCC; he saw it primarily as a substitute for the banned protest movements. "It voiced the concerns of the African people at the very time when our parties were banned and our leaders silenced in political detention."[96]

However, the RCC's hopes were soon to be severely tested. Bishop Ralph Dodge of the United Methodist Church (UMC), the first president of the RCC, was issued deportation orders in July 1964. This direct attack on the United Methodist Church triggered a grassroots response from the UMC members, which took state law enforcement agents by surprise. According to Muzorewa, police, used to fighting riotous mobs, were "startled to find churchwomen in their blue and red uniforms, men with blue sashes . . . and black-suited clergy with clerical collars demonstrating."[97]

The churches lost; Bishop Dodge was compelled to leave. Four years later, at UMC's 1968 quadrennial conference in Botswana, Muzorewa was elected bishop, becoming the first black bishop of any denomination in Southern Rhodesia. Although his predecessor, Bishop Dodge, had been active in politics, it was clear that the election of an African as head of one of the country's major denominations had effectively introduced a new factor in church-state politics. Muzorewa's role as a spiritual leader could not be separated from the fact that he was a member of the repressed African majority. His passion for ministry was therefore closely linked to his passion for political change: "I wanted our people to be liberated from over eighty years of colonialism and the implication that Africans are by nature inferior . . . I wanted them to realize that getting a good life was not the exclusive right and privilege of white people."[98]

The opportunity for Muzorewa to bridge the gap between the churches and politics came in 1971 when British Prime Minister Sir Alec Douglas-Home and Ian Smith attempted to legitimize a constitution that purported to resolve the franchise question. The only question was whether the black majority would accept it. The Pierce Commission was set up to collect black opinion on the matter.

The new constitutional proposals introduced three voters' rolls. There was to be a European roll and an African "higher roll" that required an annual income of at least Z$1,800 or property worth over Z$3,600. If one had four years of secondary school, then the income requirement was reduced to Z$1,200 and the property value brought down to Z$2,400. Needless to say, most of the African population could not meet these financial requirements. The educational requirement was also outrageous, considering that in 1971 there were only 414 blacks with six years of secondary school and 2,545 with four years of high school.[99]

The "lower roll" demanded either an annual income of over Z$600 or property worth over Z$1,100. However, people with two years of education could be admitted to the lower roll if they had an annual income of Z$300 or property worth Z$600. Additional compromises were made for people over thirty years of age with a limited amount of education. They could also be added to this list. The voters on the first roll, which included very few blacks, would vote for fifty members of parliament. The voters on the lower roll, which would be larger and dominated by Africans, would vote for only sixteen members of parliament.

Although the majority of the Africans were opposed to anything less than universal suffrage, they lacked a united political voice with which to challenge the new constitutional proposals. The vacuum created by the banning and restriction of black organizations suddenly became extraordinarily acute during this crisis: "Our people . . . wanted to fight this betrayal and frustrate it, yet . . . There was no political party to act as a vehicle of our struggle and the old nationalist leaders were . . . in prisons and detention camps.[100]

The link between the role of the churches and the activation of civil society organizations manifested itself in an intriguing manner during this crisis. Individuals who had served on the executive committees of ZAPU and ZANU took advantage of the relative political freedom that accompanied the commission hearings to create the African National Council (ANC) through which to campaign against the proposed constitution. But instead of leading the ANC themselves, they turned to church leaders. Muzorewa says he was taken by surprise when the group that formed the ANC asked him to serve as its president. Canaan Banana, another radical Methodist minister, was elected vice president. According to Muzorewa, the core group that formed the ANC assured him that its creation had been endorsed by the jailed nationalist leaders Ndabaningi Sithole and Joshua Nkomo.[101]

What is clear from these events is that repressed civil society organizations themselves recognize the churches as Bayart's "zone of liberty" and will, if necessary, graft themselves to the churches until the public arena is liberated. In sum, they use the relative liberty allowed to the churches.

Muzorewa's leadership role during this crisis greatly boosted his political standing. Speaking at a 16 December 1970 press conference, Muzorewa described the proposed constitution as a "vicious and subtle device" designed to appease the international community without providing any real change in the political conditions of the Africans. Acceptance of the proposals would be a "betrayal of the Africans, dead, living, yet to be born." Muzorewa made it clear the proposals provided no basis for any meaningful negotiation. "We cannot be vendors of our heritage and rights."[102]

Muzorewa and Banana tapped into church resources to mount a nationwide campaign. The RCC produced pamphlets in the country's three major languages (English, Ndebele, and Shona) which showed why the Africans should refuse to accept the constitutional proposal. In December, the RCC voted twenty-nine to nine against the proposals.

Therefore, by the time the Pierce Commission began to gather public reactions, the situation was already tense. The commission arrived in Rhodesia on 11 January 1972. The following day a man was killed in a disturbance. By the end of the month at least thirteen blacks had been killed and many blacks and whites injured in mass demonstrations. Many had been detained, including former Rhodesian Prime Minister Garfield Todd and his daughter, Judith Todd. The treasurer of the African National Council and his wife were also arrested. The reaction of the black majority seemed to support Bishop Muzorewa's position that the proposals as were "both an insult to the African people and a prescription for a bloodbath."[103]

The Pierce Commission left Rhodesia in March; its conclusions were finally announced in May. The proposals were rejected. Africans had won a major victory against the white minority state. This victory elevated Muzorewa's standing in Zimbabwean politics. He seemed to be living up to his pledge to fight against the Rhodesian political system.[104]

Having won this victory, the ANC now faced the challenge of re-maining an active opposition movement in an environment where such movements were not permitted to exist. This limited what the ANC could do and say. Muzorewa's position was that the ANC was "too important to risk proscription." According to him, the ANC leadership decided to distance itself from the then Lusaka-based liberation organizations and even welcomed broadcasts from Lusaka that were critical of the ANC.[105]

In October 1974, South African Prime Minister John Vorster, realizing that the imminent independence of Mozambique and Angola would ef-fectively change the balance of power in the region, announced a new strategy. South Africa would now promote a negotiated settlement in Zimbabwe rather than support a military conquest by the guerrillas. Vor-ster's rationale for this change in strategy was that the "price of con-frontation would be high, too high for Southern Africa." President Kaunda welcomed Vorster's apparent change of heart as "the voice of reason which Africa and the rest of the world have waited for."[106]

The influence of South Africa on Zimbabwe's internal politics soon became very clear. A month after Vorster's announcement, Smith quickly released Nkomo and Sithole from jail and put them, together with Muzorewa, on a chartered plane to Lusaka where Kaunda was sup-posed to monitor a unity agreement among the divided nationalist or-ganizations. *This* secret state-financed trip for Muzorewa and the jailed nationalist leaders resulted in a unity statement agreed upon due to the influence of Kaunda. The United African National Council (UANC), an umbrella organization, was set up and Bishop Muzorewa was elected president.[107]

The UANC was doomed from the beginning. The unity agreement was little more than a piece of paper. The ethnic divide between the Ndebele under Nkomo and the Shona under Mugabe was too deep to be dealt with so easily. The nationalist leaders, under friendly but firm pres-sure from Kaunda on the one side and hostile threats from Smith on the other, had little option but to endorse the unity agreement.

In reality, there was little unity between the factions of the liberation organizations. This severely undermined Muzorewa's ability to negotiate with Smith. Muzorewa himself gives the impression that Nkomo was conducting secret talks with Smith in the hope of making an independent agreement that would position Nkomo as the potential president of a transitional government. Following a prolonged power struggle with Nkomo, Muzorewa expelled Nkomo from the ANC. Muzorewa's move may have been justified, but it was miscalculated. Muzorewa did not realize that Nkomo enjoyed greater Frontline support and that even Smith saw Nkomo as a more powerful force.

Nkomo defied Muzorewa's expulsion and organized an ANC congress in September 1975 at which he was elected president. Muzorewa insinuated that Nkomo's gathering was financed by Smith. He said Nkomo "suddenly" had over twenty cars with which to organize the congress. Since the law did not permit African groups to hold open-air meetings, he claimed the state provided tents and chairs for Nkomo's meetings. Of the four thousand who allegedly attended this meeting, over two thousand came from Matebeleland, Nkomo's home region. To reach the four thousand, Muzorewa claimed the state "instructed policemen in plain clothes, their families, and other civil servants to attend."[108]

The conflict between Muzorewa and the leaders of the nationalist organizations reveals that it is perilous for church leaders to attempt to play what appears to be a permanent role in politics. As long as churches and church leaders are seen as performing a substitutionary function, their role is welcomed by the leaders of the political opposition. But once they appear to have political ambitions, they get caught up in the continuous struggle for power characteristic of all political movements. In this regard, Bishop Tutu can be said to have been more astute than Bishop Muzorewa. Tutu made it clear that he had no direct political ambitions and that he was "no Bishop Muzorewa."[109]

However, the case can be made that Bishop Muzorewa did not set out to gain political power. Until 1971, Bishop Muzorewa was a church-based political activist. His role in campaigning against the Smith-Home constitutional proposals was clearly still substitutionary. Muzorewa saw the ANC as a civil society organization whose objective was to oppose an unjust political system using peaceful means. Muzorewa did not see any conflict between his role as church leader and his role in the ANC. "As leader both of the church and the ANC, we have taken the line that we are part of a non-violent organization and we follow non-violent methods."[110]

In 1974, when all the nationalist organizations met in Lusaka and eventually signed the unity accord, Muzorewa was willing to step down. "In fact I went outside for more than three hours while the question of leadership was being discussed."[111] The participants at this meeting, including both Nkomo and Mugabe, opted for Muzorewa. "I feel the tallest man in the world," said Muzorewa during the signing ceremony.[112]

After 1974, Muzorewa began to see himself as the "tallest man" in Zimbabwe. Muzorewa, perhaps naively, perceived himself as the legitimate leader of the organizations fighting for Zimbabwean liberation. His election in Lusaka may have persuaded him that he was the only leader who could maintain unity between all the factions seeking power in Zimbabwe. The ethnic division and the power struggles he witnessed firsthand as he interacted with the nationalist organizations confirmed his fears. The assassinations that took place among the nationalist groups further confirmed the need for Muzorewa's intervention. For example, in 1975 Herbert Chitepo, a leading ZANU figure, was assassinated in Lusaka. It soon became clear that his assassination was planned from within the nationalist organizations. Other assassinations had been planned to include Muzorewa, Nkomo, and Sithole. Muzorewa was moved to tears: "I wept for Zimbabwe, not because I was one of those to be eliminated, but because . . . tribal bickering and murders weakened our unity."[113]

Therefore, what Muzorewa saw and experienced among the exiled organizations may have persuaded him that as a church leader he had a higher obligation to spare Zimbabweans from such leadership. His distrust of the nationalist leaders became most apparent during the 1980 elections. The events leading to these elections and the role of the churches are discussed below.

In 1976, Britain arranged more talks between the nationalist movements and Smith's government. The talks failed and the nationalist organizations opted to step up the war. They made significant gains, although at high cost. Many churches and church institutions were severely affected by the guerilla war.[114] This environment placed an extra burden on Muzorewa. "What frightened me most and worried me sick was that the black population looked to me to do something about the situation."[115]

Therefore, in November 1977, in response to a Smith initiative, Muzorewa and leaders of two other nationalist organizations began to negotiate with Smith for a new constitutional arrangement that would be acceptable to both whites and blacks. A fragile settlement was finally reached in March 1978. The agreement provided for universal suffrage, set 31 December 1978 as the date for the introduction of majority rule, and immediately ushered in a transitional government with Muzorewa as prime minister. Muzorewa and others were persuaded that this would lead to a cease-fire.[116]

The settlement was met with relentless international criticism. Several criticisms were raised: (1) The constitution reserved twenty-eight seats out of one hundred for the minority white population; (2) Muzorewa and others swore to uphold the inherited constitution of the white government: (3) Decisions of the three-person executive council were to be made by consensus, thus giving Smith enough power to block any decision: (4) The existing white parliament would continue to function though the transition period.[117]

The most damaging aspect of this settlement was that it excluded the nationalist organizations from the transitional process. But with one of its own top leaders now directly involved in the controversial settlement, the Christian community was understandably in a quandary. The RCC adopted a particularistic approach; it opted to continue addressing the human rights issues by calling for the unconditional release of political prisoners and for the government to stop detaining people without trial. However, the RCC was fully aware that a solution that excluded movements in exile would not be effective. One of its statements observed that "a conference of all interested parties is required" and urged Muzorewa's government to meet with "all others" and try to find a solution.[118]

The wishes of the churches were granted through the 1980 Lancaster House talks, which resulted from a British Commonwealth conference held in Lusaka. The nationalist Patriotic Front (PF) and the Smith-Muzorewa government were brought back to the negotiation table. In contrast to some of the leaders of the Anglican Church, to whom the Lancaster House talks were an "appeasement . . . of armed marauders,"[119] the RCC reacted positively to the talks and sent representatives to London to help foster reconciliation between the rival organizations.

After a lengthy and fragile negotiation process, the Lancaster House talks produced a compromise transitional constitution that was more or less acceptable to ZAPU, ZANU, ANC, and the Rhodesian Front.[120] Elections were set for April 1980.

During the election campaign, Muzorewa labeled ZAPU and ZANU as communist groups and declared the election a choice between democratic politics and a one-party Marxist state.[121] Muzorewa also used his incumbent position to his advantage. "As prime minister with the evident backing of the white community, he had access to the media and the full force of the bureaucracy."[122] However, the election results showed that Muzorewa's decision to cooperate with the government had made him the least favored candidate in the process. He received approximately 8.3 percent of the votes, and his party three seats out of eighty.[123]

Muzorewa's greatest mistake (which Tutu later tactfully avoided in South Africa) was to assume that the opportunity afforded to the churches and church leaders to play a significant role in politics during times of repression is tantamount to a mandate for long-term involvement. This assumption was simply wrong. The masses expect the churches and church leaders to assume political roles as a substitutionary arrangement; as soon as civil society is liberated, church leaders who remain in the political arena and assume partisan positions lose their legitimacy.

The Muzorewa experience also reveals the gap between the political idealism that church leaders often bring into the political arena and the realities of political practice. It takes more than good ideas to win an election and consolidate dominion. In other words, the political process usually eliminates the well-motivated in favor of the astute, the idealists in favor of the realists.

Muzorewa's idealism is reflected in his picture of the head of state desirable for an independent Zimbabwe. Writing in 1978, two years before Zimbabwe's independence and nearly twenty years before the rise of the pro-democracy movement that swept across the continent, Muzorewa's ideal of a president was a person who could tolerate criticism. Muzorewa did not want to see a president in Zimbabwe who would "see plots behind every bush," and use such plots as an excuse to oppress opponents. The ideal head of state was one who could be removed through the electoral process and "gracefully step and settle down to private life." Finally, Muzorewa wished Zimbabwe would have a head of state who is "mature enough to know that he is not God."[124]

Muzorewa also had a vision of a political system in which people could opt for multiparty politics if they so chose. Muzorewa said those who insist on a one-party system do so "either because they have lost touch with the masses or because they were afraid of the opposition."[125] Muzorewa's thinking was prophetic. It was not long before the ruling ZANU-PF was pitted against a growing opposition movement.

CHURCHES AND POLITICS AFTER 1980

The coming of independence in 1980 marked a change in church-state relations in Zimbabwe. With the franchise question resolved, individual liberties restored, and civil society liberated, the churches had no immediate cause for a confrontation with the state. The churches reverted to the more traditional issues of evangelization. For example, in 1980, the ZCC organized a symposium on evangelism that attracted over one hundred participants from about eighteen denominations. The symposium examined how Christianity could be reconciled with traditional religion.[126] This was a departure from the earlier church conferences and publications that had almost always addressed political concerns and called for political change. It is clear that the churches were relatively content with the new political system and had decided to focus their energies on matters other than political affairs.

The result was a distinct shift in church-state relations from the confrontational model to the more or less collaborative and complementary models. The churches recognized the state's legitimacy and were willing to cooperate with the state in its efforts to rebuild the war-ravaged country.

For its part, the state also recognized the churches as a legitimate and relatively powerful constituent of civil society, and, despite its Marxist inclinations, appealed to the churches for cooperation. Mugabe had astutely realized long before independence that the state would need the support of the churches in order to achieve its goals. In an interview he gave in Maputo in 1978, Mugabe not only acknowledged the role of the churches as agents of development, but also recognized their political influence in society. "The churches by and large are the dominant influence among our people," he said.[127]

Therefore, when Mugabe's new government produced reconstruction and development programs, the churches showed a willingness to cooperate. The Catholic Church, endowed with more resources than most Protestant churches (and the denomination to which Mugabe's family belonged), led the way. Through its development service units, the Catholic Church initiated and administered a nationwide development program. The Catholic Church's programs ranged from literacy to agriculture to schools and hospitals.[128]

The member churches of the ZCC also took the government's development initiative seriously. Bishop Shiri, then president of the ZCC, challenged the churches to help the new government in its rebuilding and reconstruction initiatives. "We can play a very important role if we get involved," he said.[129]

The ZCC developed a Reconstruction Aid Appeal, asking for Z$5.2 million, which it submitted to the World Council of Churches (WCC). However, for a variety of reasons, including some doubts about the ZCC's ability to handle finances and some administrative problems, ZCC's appeal for international funding was not very successful. Only Z$2 million was pledged.[130]

It is clear, therefore, that soon after 1980 the churches withdrew from the arena of political confrontation with the state, and developed collaborative and complementary relations with it. It is important to note that church-state harmony can only be measured in relative terms. Since the churches always constitute a potential threat to the state, conflict can never be totally absent. Sporadic confrontation will occur. For example, in 1981, conflict occurred between President Canaan Banana and the ZCC. Banana, himself a minister, visited the WCC in Geneva where he was told that some churches abroad had chosen not to support the state's development programs because of concerns that the state was Marxist. Since it was Muzorewa who had accused Mugabe and others of being Marxist during the 1980 campaign, Banana probably concluded that Muzorewa, who was again a member of the executive council of the ZCC, was behind the smear campaign.

Upon returning to Africa, Canaan Banana attacked the ZCC for its failure to support the new government.[131] However, this development must be seen for what it was: a conflict between political rivals who happened to be church leaders as well. It does not reflect a change in the general pattern of collaborative and complementary church-state relations that characterized Zimbabwe from 1980 to about 1985. The point is that the conflict between the rivals was not linked to state repression.

CHURCH AND STATE AFTER 1985

Although there was relative harmony between church and state after 1980, this harmony was still fragile. As long as the churches supported government programs and avoided expressly political issues, it could be maintained. And as long as political dissent could be expressed by other groups in civil society, such as opposition parties, the churches were not under particular pressure to assume this function. But when the state begins to repress the other groups, the churches were invariably drawn into direct church-state conflict.

The potential for church-state conflict was first apparent in 1982 when the alliance between Nkomo's ZAPU and Mugabe's ZANU collapsed. Arms caches were discovered in ZAPU-controlled areas. The government accused ZAPU of planning an armed rebellion. Nkomo was expelled from the cabinet and forced to flee into exile. Nkomo's supporters, disappointed and bitter, and some of them still armed, expressed their dissent by returning to the bush and resuming the guerilla war. The government, perhaps legitimately fearing that South Africa would arm the rebels as it had RENAMO in Mozambique and UNITA in Angola, responded with overwhelming military force. The brutality with which the troops allegedly conducted this operation led to an outcry from the churches. At Easter 1983, Catholic bishops issued a statement entitled "Reconciliation Is Still Possible." Said the bishops: "Violent reaction against dissident activity has brought about the maiming and death of hundreds and hundreds of innocent people who are neither dissidents nor collaborators." Mugabe was reportedly "stung" by this statement and "reacted with a sharp counter-attack."[132]

The conflict between Nkomo and Mugabe continued for at least four years. In 1985, Nkomo accused government troops of killing hundreds of his supporters. Muzorewa supported Nkomo.[133] The Catholic Church again condemned the behavior of Mugabe's troops.[134] The conflict was finally resolved in 1987. A unity agreement was reached between Nkomo and Mugabe, leading to the formation of ZANU-PF as an independent party. In the same year, Zimbabwe moved from a parliamentary to a presidential system with Mugabe as president.

Therefore, the initial euphoria with which the churches had met independence died out by the late 1980s. The churches were now poised to challenge the state's moves to liquidate political opposition. These were opposed by the churches, particularly by the Catholic bishops, because it was seen as a threat to the liberties that Zimbabweans had gained in 1980. "Nothing in the Constitution should put at risk the freedom of expression and freedom of assembly of the people," said a 1989 statement issued by the bishops.[135]

The state did not take this opposition kindly. In his 1990 New Year's address to the nation, Mugabe described those who opposed the one-party state as "people with little minds" who were misinterpreting such a change as a "threat to democracy" and cited the Catholic Church as one such group.[136]

Another area of conflict between the churches and the state has been the increased corruption that has come to be associated with the government. In 1989, the *Chronicle* newspaper revealed mass corruption among many of Mugabe's government ministers and many members of parliament. The ensuing public scandal forced many state officials to resign. The government responded by dismissing Geoff Nyarota, the newspaper's editor. Nyarota was threatened with arrest for refusing to disclose his sources.[137] Such incidents created concern about possible human rights violations by the state, and in 1992 the churches joined with the country's legal community to form a human rights watchdog organization.[138] It is also evident that the government has lost its initial popularity. The state closed the University of Zimbabwe following antigovernment protests by students and banned any demonstrations by the labor movement. But opposition is on the rise and includes the country's financial and industrial magnates. As one report puts it, "More businesslike than students or union members, the captains of industry and commerce have not taken to the streets but they have thrown their weight behind groups looking for a viable alternative to the Mugabe government."[139] There is no evidence that the churches support a particular opposition movement, but there is no doubt that they now oppose the ruling party.

The erosion of the government's popularity is also revealed by the apathy shown toward the activities of the ruling party—a trend apparently welcomed by the churches, whose members "had their homes burnt and looted because they were known as churchgoers not prepared to attend party meetings."[140] There also seems to be an underlying competition for public support between the churches and the ruling party. For example, the fact that two hundred and fifty thousand people voluntarily gathered for the 1988 papal visit "did not go unnoticed by politicians who . . . have trouble getting people to attend party meetings."[141] The decline of ZANU seems to be celebrated by the churches: "There are fewer political meetings today, but the churches continue to be full."[142] President Mugabe sees the political apathy as a short-lived phenomenon. Says he: "Apathy there certainly is but what some people do not quite know is that apathy is not antipathy but a mere attitude of temporary disinterest."[143]

However, the longer the ruling Party has stayed in power and continued to further gag the opposition and stifle society, the more church-state relations have deteriorated. The Roman Catholic Church's Justice and Peace Commission continues to issue biting press releases again actions of the state—exposing everything from human rights abuses by government agents, to the plight of the poor, to the injustices of excessive land acquisition by those in power who seize the properties of white Zimbabweans illegally. The Protestant churches, through the ZCC, mounted a campaign to change the constitution which they claimed gave too much power to the head of state. Church leaders and church organizations have also been relentless in criticizing the Mugabe government's decision to send "peacekeeping" troops into the civil-war torn Republic of Congo. The role of these troops in bringing peace is not clear; neither is Zimbabwe's strategic interest in the conflict. The situation in Zimbabwe in 2001 is amazingly similar to how it was in Zambia in early 1991. As one observer put it, "It seems Zimbabweans [got] a cue from Zambians."[144]

NOTES

1. In this study I will use the name Zimbabwe when referring to this country. However, it should be noted that Zimbabwe was known as Southern Rhodesia or simply as Rhodesia until 1980.

2. Abel Muzorewa, *Rise up and Walk: The Autobiography of Bishop Tendekai Muzorewa*, Norman E. Thomas ed. (Nashville, TN: Abingdon, 1978), 90.

3. All the above statistics are taken from Patrick Johnstone, *Operation World: The Day by Day Guide to Praying for the World* (Grand Rapids, MI: Zondervan Publishing House, 1993), 598. My estimate of "followers" is a combination of "members" and "affiliates" because in Africa the distinction is not critical. Membership records are often out of date; people often establish "membership" by attending the services of one group over a period of time.

4. For this perspective, see Paul Gifford, *The Religious Right in Southern Africa* (Harare: Baobab Books Publications, 1988).

5. Frans Maritz, "Church-State Relations in The Dutch Reformed Church (NGK) in Zimbabwe: A Case Study," in *Church and State in Zimbabwe*, ed. Carl F. Hallencreutz and Ambrose M. Moyo (Harare: Mambo Press, 1988), 347–360.

6. Carl F. Hallencreutz, "A Council in Crossfire: ZCC 1964–1980," in *Church and State in Zimbabwe*, ed. Hallencreutz and Moyo, 56.

7. Solomon M. Nkiwane, *The Churches' Role as Agents of Peace and Development: Case Study—Zimbabwe* (Uppsala, Sweden: Life and Peace Institute, 1992), 13.

8. Ibid., 15.

9. Ibid., 13.

10. Quoted by Terence O. Ranger, *The African Voice in Southern Rhodesia 1989–1930* (Evanston, IL: Northwestern University Press, 1970), 18.

11. Adrian Hastings, *A History of African Christianity 1950–1975* (New York: Cambridge University Press, 1979), 21.

12. Quoted by Ian Linden, *The Catholic Church and the Struggle for Zimbabwe* (London: Longman, 1980), 9.

13. Ibid., 13.

14. Roger Paeden, "The Contribution of the Epworth Mission Settlement to African Development," *Themes in the Christian History of Central Africa*, ed. Terence O. Ranger and John Weller (Los Angeles: University of California Press, 1975), 135.

15. Linden, *The Catholic Church and the Struggle for Zimbabwe*, 31.

16. Ibid., 13.

17. Paeden, 147.

18. See "Conflict over Land: White Farmers and the Black Government," and "Conflict over Land: Communal Farmers versus Squatters," in Jeffrey

Herbst, *State Politics in Zimbabwe* (Los Angeles: University of California Press, 1990), 37–81.

19. Linden, *The Catholic Church and the Struggle for Zimbabwe*, 13.

20. These articles appeared in the *Rhodesian Herald* and are quoted in Ibid., 14.

21. Ranger, *The African Voice in Southern Rhodesia*, 16.

22. Linden, *The Catholic Church and the Struggle for Zimbabwe*, 26.

23. Leonard Kapungu, *Rhodesia: The Struggle for Freedom* (New York: Orbis Books, 1974), 84.

24. Ibid.

25. Both quotations in Ranger, *The African Voice in Southern Rhodesia*, 22.

26. Kapungu, 84.

27. Linden, *The Catholic Church and the Struggle for Zimbabwe*, 25.

28. Chengai J. Zvobgo, "The African Franchise Question," in *Church and State in Zimbabwe*, ed. Hallencreutz and Moyo, 29.

29. Ibid., 29–33.

30. Ibid., 29.

31. Murray Steele, " 'With Hope Unconquered . . . ': Arthur Shearly Cripps, 1869–1952" *Themes in the Christian History of Central Africa*, 152–174.

32. Zvobgo, 31.

33. Ibid.

34. Ibid., 32.

35. Jean-François Bayart, "La Fonction Politique des Eglises au Cameroon," *Revue Francaise de Science Politique* 3 (3 June 1973): 514.

36. Zvobgo, 33.

37. E. S. Atieno-Odhiambo, "Origins of the Zimbabwe Problem, 1888–1923," in *Zimbabwe Now* (Rex Collins: London, 1972), 22.

38. Zvobgo, 34.

39. Ibid., 34.

40. Ibid., 35.

41. Ibid., 37.

42. Quoted in Zvogbo, 35.

43. Quoted in Ibid., 36.

44. Ranger, *The African Voice*, 16.

45. Terence O. Ranger, *Are We Not Also Men? The Samkange Family and African Politics in Zimbabwe 1920–64* (Portsmouth, NH: Heinemann, 1995), 88–89.

46. Ibid., 89.

47. Ibid., 90.

48. Ibid., 93.

49. Ibid., 98.

50. Ibid., 106.

51. Ibid., 95.

52. Ibid., 119–123.

53. A. R. Wilkinson, quoted in Michael Raeburn, *Black Fire: Accounts of the Guerilla War in Rhodesia* (London: Julian Friedmann Publishers, 1978), 1.

54. Ibid., 4.

55. Hastings, *History of African Christianity*, 92.

56. Ibid., 143.

57. Ibid., 140.

58. Nkiwane, 19.

59. For a profile, see "Smith Himself," in Kenneth Young, *Rhodesia and Independence* (New York: James Heinemann, 1967), 108–128.

60. Ian Hancock, *The Liberals, Moderates and Radicals in Rhodesia 1953–1980* (New York: St. Martin's Press, 1984), 194.

61. Young, *Rhodesia and Independence*, 139.

62. Linden, *The Catholic Church and the Struggle for Zimbabwe*, 87.

63. Kapungu, 63.

64. Herbst, 27–28.

65. Herbst, 28.

66. Hastings, *History of African Christianity*, 216.

67. Ibid.

68. Lapsley, "Anglican Church and State from UDI in 1965 until the Independence of Zimbabwe in 1980," in *Church and State in Zimbabwe*, ed. Hallencreutz and Moyo, 116.

69. Ibid., 117.

70. For accounts of the guerilla activities, see Michael Raeburn, *Black Fire*.

71. Lapsley, 122.

72. Ibid., 123.

73. Ibid., 119–120.

74. Hastings, *History of African Christianity*, 142.

75. Hallencreutz, "A Council in Crossfire," 60.

76. Kapungu, 92.

77. Hallencreutz, "A Council in Crossfire," 63.

78. Nkiwane, 19.

79. Hallencreutz, "A Council in Crossfire," 62.

80. Hastings, *History of African Christianity*, 216.

81. For more comprehensive studies, see Ian Linden, *The Catholic Church and the Struggle for Zimbabwe* (London: Longman, 1980); and Enda McDonagh, *Church and Politics: From Theology to a Case History of Zimbabwe* Notre Dame, IN: University of Notre Dame Press, 1980).

82. Cited McDonagh, 80.

83. Kapungu, 9.

84. Ibid., 87.

85. Ibid., 89.

86. Ibid., 89.

87. Ibid., 93.

88. Catholic Commission for Justice and Peace in Zimbabwe, *The Man in the Middle: Torture, Resettlement and Eviction*. Harare: Catholic Commission for Justice and Peace, 1975.

89. Kapungu, 95.

90. Ibid., 96.

91. Hallencreutz, "A Council in Crossfire," 67–68.

92. Muzorewa, *Rise up and Walk*, 17.

93. Ibid., 17–18.

94. Ibid., 49.

95. Ibid., 55.

96. Ibid., 59.

97. Ibid., 59.

98. Ibid., 68.

99. Hallencreutz, "A Council in Crossfire," 89.

100. Muzorewa, *Rise up and Walk*, 94.

101. Ibid.

102. Ibid., 95.

103. Raeburn, *Black Fire*, 11.

104. Kapungu, 89.

105. Muzorewa, *Rise up and Walk*, 119.

106. Ibid., 139.

107. *Statement Issued in Salisbury by the Newly Formed African National Council at 1600 Hours on Thursday 12 December, 1974.*

108. Muzorewa, *Rise up and Walk*, 169.

109. Desmond Tutu, *Crying in the Wilderness* (London: Mowbray, 1986), 33.

110. Abel Muzorewa, "The Role of the ANC," *Zimbabwe Now* (London: Rex Collers, 1972), 122.

111. Muzorewa, *Rise Up and Walk*, 143.

112. Ibid., 143.

113. Ibid.

114. For good case studies, see Michael Bourdillon and Paul Gumdani, "Rural Christians and the Zimbabwe Liberation War: A Case Study"; and Ngwabi Bhebhe, "The Evangelical Lutheran Church in Zimbabwe and the War of Liberation, 1975–1980," both in *Church and State in Zimbabwe*, ed. Hallencreutz and Moyo, 147–194.

115. Hallencreutz, "A Council in Crossfire," 85.

116. *A Rhodesian Settlement? Analysis of an Agreement Signed by Prime Minister Ian Smith of Rhodesia, The Reverend Ndabaningi Sithole, Bishop Abel Muzorewa, and Senators Jeremiah Chirau on March 3 1978: A Staff Report to the Committee on Foreign Relations, United States Senate.*

117. For a critical analysis of this settlement see International Defence and

Aid Fund, *Smith's Settlement: Events in Zimbabwe since 3rd March 1978* (London: International Defence and Aid Fund, 1978).

118. Hallencreutz, "A Council in Crossfire," 95.

119. Lapsley, 124.

120. For a complete account of these talks, see Jeffrey David, *The Peace in Southern Africa: The Lancaster House Conference on Rhodesia, 1979* (Boulder, CO: Westview Press, 1984).

121. Henry Wiseman and Alistair M. Taylor, *From Rhodesia to Zimbabwe: The Politics of Transition* (New York: Pergamon Press, 1981), 22.

122. Ibid., 22.

123. Ibid., 23.

124. Muzorewa, *Rise Up and Walk*, 256–257.

125. Ibid., 255.

126. Hallencreutz, "A Council in Crossfire," 259–263.

127. Janice McLaughlin, " 'We Did It for Love': Refugees and Religion in the Camps in Mozambique and Zambia during Zimbabwe's Liberation Struggle," *Church and State in Zimbabwe*, 137.

128. Paul H. Gundani, "The Catholic Church and National Development in Independent Zimbabwe," *Church and State in Zimbabwe*, 215–249.

129. Hallencreutz, "A Council in Crossfire," 254.

130. Ibid., 255–257.

131. Ibid., 268.

132. *New People: The African Church Open to the World* (May–June 1990), 6.

133. For reports of these events, see *Newsweek* (18 March 1985), 41; *Time* (18 March 1985), 38; *National Review* (5 April 1985), 63.

134. Roger Parker, "A Tangled Revolution," *Commonweal* 113 (28 February 1986), 107–10.

135. *New People: The African Church Open to the World.* (May–June, 1990), 7.

136. Foreign Broadcasting Information Service, (3 January 1990).

137. Ibid. (25 May 1993).

138. *Africa Report* (July–August 1992).

139. Ibid.

140. *New People* (May–June 1990), 7.

141. Ibid.

142. Ibid.

143. Foreign Broadcast Information Service (29 June 1992).

144. *Africa Report* (July–August 1992).

Chapter Four _____

Churches and Change in South Africa

Perhaps nowhere in Africa were church-state relations as turbulent as they were in South Africa in the last four decades of the twentieth century. This chapter examines the evolution of church-state relations and the role of the churches in South African politics from 1960 to the end of the century. This includes South Africa's most volatile years, spanning the banning of the nationalist movements and the arrest of their leaders to the abolition of apartheid, the release of black leaders, and the un-banning of the African National Congress (ANC). These changes led to the election of Nelson Mandela as South Africa's first black president in 1994.

The theoretical framework guiding the chapters in this book has been discussed in the introduction. The primary argument is that churches in Africa are periodically drawn into confrontation with the state when they take upon themselves the "expressly political functions" of the repressed elements of society. African governments frequently adopt a variety of methods to expand and consolidate their control over society, for example, banning and intimidating groups and movements that seek to bring about societal changes. During such periods, the churches, which for a variety of reasons the state cannot totally repress, emerge as the only element of civil society with the organization and leadership resources needed to challenge the state as "substitutes" for the banned groups. This leads to a direct confrontation between the churches and the state.

However, the framework also accommodates the reality that churches are not monolithic and thus they do not respond en masse to the vacuum caused by the banning of opposition groups. This was particularly crucial in South Africa during the apartheid period when state-societal relations were defined largely by race. As will be shown, the response of the churches in general reflected the racial division of the society. Predominantly black churches and black church leaders, effectively represented by the South African Council of Churches (SACC), responded to the vacuum created by the banning of black nationalist movements by taking over these functions, and earned a reputation as the "ANC at prayer."

At first, the predominantly white denominations responded to increased state repression of the black majority with overt justification of the apartheid system and later with an ambivalent reevaluation of their position. But it was not until the demise of apartheid was imminent that the Afrikaner-dominated denominations took the antiapartheid position that earlier on would have been considered confrontational to the state but by then (in the face of white extremism that was a threat to the National Party government) was actually welcomed by the state.

This chapter begins with the historical background that is necessary for a better understanding of the evolution of church-state relations in South Africa. Particularly important is the role of Christianity in the survival of the Afrikaner community and its later rise to political dominance from 1948 to 1990. The chapter also explores the impact of Christianity on the indigenous peoples and examines the role of Christianity in the development of the nationalist movements that were eventually banned in the 1960s. It then employs Bayart's framework to examine the response of the churches to the increased state repression that began in the 1960s and ended with the demise of apartheid and the liberation of civil society in the 1990s.

CHRISTIANITY IN SOUTH AFRICA

South Africa's history is one of racial conflict.[1] The Portuguese explorer Bartholomew Diaz first reached what he called the "Cape of Good Hope" in 1446. But it was not until 1652 that the first white settlements of the Dutch East India Company appeared along the coast. Before long, more white immigrant families arrived, and the settler community expanded.

Since most of these settlers were of Dutch origin, the Dutch Reformed Church (DRC) became the earliest form of organized Christianity in the Cape. The first DRC minister arrived in 1665 and his task was almost exclusively to serve the white settler community, in part because the indigenous people were considered heathens and according to the dictates of the Synod of Dort of 1618, heathens were not to be baptized.[2]

It is not surprising, therefore, that most white settlers considered Christianity an exclusive religion, to which nonwhites should not be admitted, and were offended by any attempt to convert the local people. This contradicts the assertion of some critics of Christianity in Africa, that whites were eager to exchange the faith for Africa's natural resources. In fact, the missionaries represented the most liberal thinking in the settler community. For example, when George Schmidt, a Moravian missionary, began work among the indigenous Khoi people in 1737, DRC ministers criticized and opposed his efforts so much that he became disheartened and left in 1744.[3]

In 1795, the British took control of the Cape. They were driven out in 1803, but regained their control of the Cape in 1806. British intervention loosened the grip of the Dutch churches and opened up South Africa to missionaries from other European backgrounds. The Moravians returned and resumed their work among the Khoi. Catholics also appeared in 1804. In 1806 the first two Catholic priests were ejected from the colony by an anti-Catholic British general. Nonetheless, the Catholic Church soon established a strong presence in South Africa.[4]

After the British had consolidated their position in the colony, a new wave of settlers immigrated to the Cape, and this led to the emergence of an English-speaking middle class served by English-speaking churches. Thus "English-speaking churches" in South Africa refers to "those churches which originated in Great Britain and use English as an official language."[5] These churches, influenced by the liberal tradition of the English in contrast to the conservative (and racist) tradition of the Afrikaners, tended to be more sympathetic to black aspirations.

The African people were receptive to the Christian message. According to government records, there were about five hundred thousand converts by 1860.[6] Some of the earliest reactions against white domination came from these African converts. In the 1890s the Ethiopian Church movement broke away from the paternalistic white churches and founded separatist all-black churches. The first such church, the Thembu Church, was started in Transkei among the Thembu people in 1884. Its founder, Nehemiah Tile, broke away from the Wesleyan Church in 1882 "after clashing with his white superiors because of his participation in political matters."[7]

These nationalist and separatist churches set a pattern that has often repeated itself in South Africa: "This pattern consists of whites misusing religion for their own benefit and blacks skeptically challenging such misuse."[8] As will be subsequently shown, the SACC later led the way in challenging the ideology of white supremacy and dominance using Christian theology.

In the 1960s the indigenous churches formed the African Independent Churches Association.[9] Later, when black leaders took over the SACC and this body emerged as the embodiment of church-based antiapartheid activity, many of the indigenous churches joined the SACC. Although in some cases the separatist churches were criticized for not being politically active enough,[10] some contemporary studies indicate that they played significant spiritual and emotional roles among the people traumatized by apartheid. For example, a 1994 study found that the healing rituals of these churches served as therapy for the poor and troubled.[11]

With British authority consolidated in the Cape, more missionary agencies based in Europe began to send their missionaries to South Africa. Soon Anglican, Lutheran, Methodist, Presbyterian, and Catholic missions were set up among the indigenous people. Out of these missionary efforts emerged the collective community of Protestants and Catholics that comprise the present-day SACC and the South Africa Bishops Conference (which has observer status with SACC and in this study will be treated mostly as an integral part of it).[12]

The coming of Christianity to South Africa is therefore synonymous with the arrival of colonialism and the rise of apartheid. However, while the mission churches were part and parcel of this racially segregated system, it is also fair to acknowledge that, at a time when Africans had no say in the system, it was the missionaries who quite often represented African interests. Many students of South African Christian history agree that "the missionaries sought on many occasions to act as the conscience of the settlers by speaking out on behalf of the indigenous people in the struggle for land, human rights and social justice."[13] It is also true that "Very often the Christian church in its mission was the first importer of ideas of freedom, independence and human rights."[14] Albert Luthuli, the founding president of the ANC, once wrote: "The mitigating feature in the gloom of those far off days was the shaft of light sunk by Christian missions, a shaft of light to which we owe our initial enlightenment."[15]

Many Africans were soon able to draw a distinction between colonialism and Christianity and were quick to employ the very teachings of the faith to confront the white establishment. Lotter observes that, in general, blacks refused to accept "dualism between their religious convictions and their political aspirations and struggle" and so "Christianity came to be an effective instrument in the comprehensive liberation of blacks in South Africa and . . . church leaders came to play a major role in the struggle against injustice in South African society."[16]

It is no coincidence therefore that when black leaders eventually took over the SACC, and more churches with black membership joined this ecumenical body, it emerged as the foremost critic of the state in South Africa, literally taking over the functions of the banned liberation movements, and, as already noted, acquiring the reputation of being the "ANC at prayer."

By the 1960s, Christianity had become a pervasive influence in South African society. Today at least seventy percent of the country's forty million people are Christian, and mostly Protestant.[17] Since ten percent of the Christian population is Catholic, the Catholic church has often participated in politics through its observer status with the Protestant SACC.[18]

The biggest mainline Protestant denominations are the Methodist Church (6,450 congregations and some 2.5 million worshipers), the Anglican Church of the Province of South Africa (1,200 congregations and about two million worshipers), and the Afrikaner DRC (1,203 congregations and 1.4 million worshipers).[19] Other significant groups include the Lutherans, Presbyterians, and Congregationalists.[20]

Another group of churches is composed of the indigenous (that is, not part of the historic ecclesiastical tradition) churches that claim a following of nearly ten million South Africans. However, although these churches have many members, their role in the politics of modern South Africa is extremely limited and will receive little attention in this chapter.

Not surprisingly, Archbishop Ndumiso Ngada of the Federal Council of African Indigenous Churches would be infuriated by this statement. Archbishop Ngada does not appreciate that the churches he represents "were and are still looked down upon as inferior, not fit to be called churches, given derogatory names such as sects, nativistic, barbaric, messianic, new religious movements and so on." But Ngada also admits that South Africa's indigenous churches "do not own any land, they have no resources, their leaders have no academic or theological qualifications. Except for very few, they are powerless in their situation." In contrast, the historic churches, he observes, have resources and their leaders are "highly educated and very powerful."[21] Therefore, while indigenous churches ought to have influence, the reality is that they do not. It is the historic churches that have emerged as a powerful political influence in contemporary South Africa.

By the late 1970s the SACC had emerged as the body representing virtually all mainline Protestant churches (the majority of the Christian population) and therefore church-state relations in South Africa revolved around SACC-state interaction.

Between 1960 and 1990 the churches in South Africa fell roughly into three categories. One category was composed of the relatively small but financially and political powerful Afrikaner churches which were supportive of the state. Then there was the much smaller, less organized, and relatively weak group of evangelical churches that in general neither affirmed nor attacked the state. And then there was the large network of mostly black churches that comprised the SACC and, during the time when black protest movements had been effectively silenced by the state, became "the only voice for political action for blacks."[22]

As the following analysis shows, three models of church-state relations emerged that more or less conform to the typologies proposed in chapter 1 of this book.

CHURCH-STATE COLLABORATION: THE DRC MODEL

The underlying argument of this study is that churches in Africa take on political functions which either affirm or challenge the state and this leads to either collaboration or confrontation. But the framework utilized in this book also acknowledges that the churches, like most elements of civil society, are not monolithic. It is not surprising therefore that one element of the collectivity of South African churches plays the function of collaborator with the apartheid regime. And based on the historical summary above, it is again no surprise that this is the predominantly Afrikaner Dutch Reformed Church bodies.

The Dutch Reformed Church (in Afrikaans, Nederduitse Gereformeerde Kerk, or NGK) was the first Christian church to be established in the Cape. DRC work began in earnest in 1665 when the first minister arrived. The DRC provided spiritual services to the small Dutch population settled in the Cape but maintained its autonomy from Dutch nationalist intentions. This became evident in 1836 when the Dutch community moved en masse from the Cape in what has come to be known as a the Great Trek: the DRC refused to bless this move which led to the birth of the other branches of the Afrikaner churches.

But as Charles Villa-Vicencio observes, the Afrikaner churches saw their primary role as "providing extensive moral and ideological support for the Afrikaner cause." Therefore, in 1948 when the Afrikaner-dominated Nationalist Party came to power and began to consolidate Afrikaner dominion by passing legislation aimed at repressing the black majority, the Afrikaner churches provided "uncompromising support for the policies of the new regime . . . and theological legitimation for apartheid legislation and maintenance of Afrikaner rule."[23]

To gain a better understanding of the complementary role these churches played, it is useful to examine the evolution of the theology of separate development. Johann Kinghorn provides an outline that illuminates four phases in the development of the DRC's position on apartheid.[24] I will employ Kinghorn's historical framework to analyze the role of the DRC in South African politics.

Nondoctrinal Segregation

According to Kinghorn's framework, from its inception in 1652 to 1927 the DRC practiced nondoctrinal segregation. In this time period, segregation "operated on a personal level and was not institutionalized. . . . There was what one might call 'natural' segregation which must not be confused with apartheid."[25] Segregation existed and was practiced by the DRC churches more as a matter of practicality and less of doctrine. Kinghorn cites language, culture, and "hygiene" as leading to the separation of black and white Christians, not theology. An 1857 synod meeting stated that it was "desirable that our members from the heathen be assimilated into existing congregations" but for the sake of the "weak" whites, it was decided that the indigenous converts would "enjoy their Christian privileges in a separate building."[26]

Therefore up to the early twentieth century, the DRC felt that racial integration was the Christian ideal, but that racially divided congregations were a necessary evil because some DRC members found it hard to mix and mingle with the indigenous people.

At a 1926 Bloemfontein conference, some of the statements of the DRC actually sounded radical and revolutionary. For example, it was stated that "it goes against Christian principles to put general constricts on the progress of natives," that it was justifiable to "attempt to uplift blacks" and that it was the "responsibility of Christians to scrupulously monitor such divisions [the races] in order to ascertain that all sections of the population be treated fairly." The conference concluded that the teachings and spirit of Christ emphasize the "divine dignity of natives as men and women created in the image of God. Thus they shall never be used as instruments to be exploited in order to enrich others."[27]

Ideological Theology

From 1927 to 1948, the DRC radically shifted its theology from non-doctrinal segregation to ideological theology. To understand how this ideological theology was conceived, it is necessary to comprehend the general Afrikaner psyche during this period. Having attained independence from Britain in 1910, the Afrikaners went on to consolidate their power base in South Africa.

However, the Afrikaners have always feared the volatile majority black population on the one side and the liberal ideas of the English-speaking community on the other. The Afrikaners were afraid of demands from the blacks for an equal portion of South Africa's wealth, which would increase the poverty of many Afrikaners. A 1929 study showed that two-thirds of whites were already living in poverty alongside black people.[28] Alarmed by this trend, the Afrikaner legislature passed laws that gave job privileges to whites.

The DRC therefore translated the fears and the accompanying legislation into a theology suitable for its constituency. The result was the emergence of a theology that positioned whites as superior and taught that this was the design of God and therefore should be respected. "Mixed marriages between higher civilized Christianized nations and lower nations militate against the Word of God," wrote one DRC minister.[29]

Even before the National Party assumed control of parliament, party leaders were already using the term "apartheid" in their parliamentary rhetoric. On 24 June 1944, during a speech in parliament, D.F.M. Malan, leader of the then opposition National Party said apartheid would "ensure the safety of the white race and of Christian civilization by the honest maintenance of the principles of apartheid and guardianship."[30]

Rationalization

According to Kinghorn's framework, the 1948 victory of the National Party marked the beginning of the period when the DRC began to rationalize and develop a doctrine out of the ideas conceptualized earlier. A 1948 DRC document stated that Christian unity was spiritual and not necessarily physical and that the idea of racial separation had a biblical basis. The document also said that white people, having a better developed culture, had a God-given responsibility to remain trustees of South Africa until such a time as black people became ready to assume total responsibility.

The DRC was therefore developing a doctrine and rationale for apartheid. The doctrine was that God made people different and therefore the idea of a multiracial and multicultural society was contrary to God's will for South Africa. The rationale for white control was that European culture had more to offer and therefore whites should take care of the weaker African people.

By 1950 the DRC had, at least officially, moved away from espousing an overtly racist position to calling for separate development of black and whites. The DRC saw apartheid as the best way to build a lofty society. "It proposes a process of development which seeks to lead each population group to its purest and speediest autonomous destination under the hand of God's gracious providence."[31]

The National Party's interests coincided with those of the DRC, leading to what Bayart would call a "unity of purpose."[32] The Dutch churches therefore became not only a spiritual base but also an ideological base for Afrikaner nationalism. G. D. Scoltz, an Afrikaner historian, admits that "Without hesitation, it can be said that it is principally due to the Church that the Afrikaner nation has not gone under . . . With the dilution of this philosophy, it [the Afrikaner nation] must inevitably disappear."[33]

Therefore, during the 1960s when the state was arresting black leaders and banning antiapartheid organizations, it had the blessings of the DRC. There were a few dissenters. In 1963 Beyers Naude, a prominent DRC minister, was compelled to leave the ministry because he accepted the position of director of the Christian Institute, a para-church network that represented black interests and was eventually banned by the state in 1977. The DRC distanced itself from the activities of the Christian Institute and chose instead to provide the state with virtually unconditional support.

Era of Revision

However, by the 1980s the DRC was beginning to pay a high cost for its collaborative role with the South African state. In 1982 the World Association for Reformed Churches—the international network of reformed churches—declared the Afrikaner pro-apartheid theology a heresy.[34] Heresy was understood as a "form of belief that makes selective use of some parts of the Christian doctrine and rejects others, so that eventually what remains is a distorted doctrine."[35] For the Afrikaner community, to be accused of heresy was troubling, in part because the Afrikaners prided themselves on their clear understanding of Scripture.

In addition, the DRC churches could not continue to deny the injustice of the system. As the injustice of apartheid become more evident, the DRC revisited its earlier positions, ushering in what Kinghorn calls the era of revision. In 1986 the DRC published a document called *Church and Society* in which it admitted, for the first time, that there was something wrong with the policy of apartheid. It had become "convinced that the application of apartheid as a political and social system which does injustice to people and which leads to one group being unjustifiably privileged above another, cannot be accepted on Christian ethical grounds."[36]

On the surface the document seemed to indicate a shift in the relations between the DRC and the state. The statement said that human dignity must be respected by the state and argued that humans had the right to a decent life, fair economic opportunities, education, and other social services and should be free to participate in politics.

While the DRC's statements indicated a new conceptualization of what a just society ought to provide, "Nowhere . . . does one find any indication that these rights are violated in South Africa."[37] In other words, although the DRC had come to a point where it could at least outline what a good society ought to look like, it was still not willing to take on what Bayart would call the "expressly political" function of directly confronting the state with these injustices. Confrontation was a function the DRC churches were not willing to assume.

It can be concluded that the DRC maintained a collaborative relationship with the state because it saw its primary ministry as that of serving the Afrikaner community rather than the total population of South Africa. DRC theology was driven by Afrikaner perceptions that the black majority was a menace that had to be contained.

In the 1980s the DRC softened its pro-apartheid position and admitted that the system was unjust, but never directly confronted the state over this injustice. "In so doing, the Afrikaans Reformed churches . . . separated themselves from all the other major churches in the country."[38]

In the late 1980s and early 1990s, several DRC leaders on various occasions finally confessed their guilt for supporting apartheid but for many this was too late. The DRC maintained the stigma of having been the only church group that openly collaborated with the state during the country's most repressive years.

LIMITED INVOLVEMENT: THE EVANGELICAL MODEL

The evangelical churches in South Africa constitute the community of churches that in terms of theology and political practice fall somewhere between the DRC and the SACC. The DRC with its Calvinistic theology and conservative politics is to the right, and the SACC with its liberal theology and radical politics is to the left. The evangelicals have held on to the Calvinistic tradition of personal piety and doctrinal purity but have not overtly supported the status quo. On occasion they have directly confronted state policies but they have never gone as far as the SACC in taking on the functions of the banned nationalist movements. The evangelicals therefore, generally speaking, reflect the limited involvement model.

The largest evangelical group in South Africa is the Apostolic Faith Mission with 2,787 congregations and some seven hundred thousand affiliates. Others include the Assemblies of God, the Baptists, the Church of the Nazarene, and the Pentecostal Holiness Church. Although relatively small when compared to the SACC member churches and the Catholic Church, the evangelical movement is growing rapidly. For example, there were only about half a million Pentecostals in 1960 but by 1990 some 2.5 million South Africans were attending Pentecostal churches.[39]

While the DRC has received attention because of its collaboration with the government, and SACC member churches have gained prominence for their confrontational stance against the state, evangelical and Pentecostal churches have not attracted as much analysis in the literature.[40] Villa-Vicencio observes that evangelicals "probably constitute the fastest growing ecclesial group in the country," but, in a comment that shows why they have received little attention in the literature, adds that they "do not overtly choose to involve themselves as institutions in the present political crisis."[41]

However, evangelicals were not necessarily an epiphenomenon in church-state relations during this period. While the Afrikaner churches were overtly supportive of the status quo, and the SACC was overtly critical of the status quo, the evangelicals adopted a limited involvement approach. It is evident that while on one hand evangelicals were hesitant to directly confront the state, they were also hesitant to directly support apartheid.

Unlike the Dutch Reformed Church, which had a coherent pro-apartheid ideology and a relatively homogenous membership, evangelicals have tended to be racially mixed and theologically ambiguous, making it hard for them to adopt a single position on church-state issues.[42] Therefore while the DRC could preach a "white" theology and the SACC a "black" theology, the evangelical theology emphasized a "body" theology.[43] In the evangelical movement, blacks and whites stayed away from divisive church-state issues and focused on personal salvation, piety, and devotion to the "word."

As long as these evangelical groups chose not to address apartheid, they enjoyed relative unity. For example, the Evangelical Fellowship of South Africa (EFSA), which began in the early 1970s as a loose network of twenty-two evangelical denominations and thirty-two para-church organizations, had three stated objectives: (1) to encourage fellowship (essentially prayers and Bible studies) across denominations; (2) to "defend" the gospel against false teachings; and (3) to advance the gospel through evangelization. EFSA did not address itself to the social problems of contemporary South Africa.[44]

Divided by Apartheid

However, by the 1980s, in part due to the mounting pressure from black members of the evangelical churches, EFSA added a fourth objective: to promote the idea that the gospel should affect behavior. As Hugh Wetmore, general secretary of EFSA, explains: "The fourth [objective] was added by EFSA in the 80s, in response to the challenge to move from an exclusively pietistic position which emphasized 'word' to a more wholistic movement which also emphasized 'deed.' "[45] The result was that some denominations left EFSA.

In October 1985 some 150 evangelical leaders gathered for an EFSA-sponsored South African Conference of Evangelical Leaders (SACEL). The "unity in the body of Christ" that previous evangelical piety had revealed soon fell apart. It soon became evident that blacks and whites lived in different worlds: blacks came out of the "daily turbulence of township unrest" while whites came from "tranquil suburbs." The conference report admitted that this "strained the ties of unity," but in typical evangelical fashion downplayed the division by claiming that "the grace of Jesus Christ prevailed as the unity in Jesus on the basis of His gospel proved stronger than the forces of polarization."[46]

A desire for unity and reconciliation rather than confrontation and polarization is the primary reason why evangelical churches did not move into the vacuum created by state repression of blacks but rather maintained a limited, often cautious position on church-state issues. However, unlike the Afrikaner churches, which were generally steadfast in their support of the state, evangelicals were quite often troubled by their lack of involvement in politics. The SACEL delegates observed the "extreme urgency of the socio-political situation in South Africa" and regretted "the failure of evangelicals to often speak out against opposition, and to work toward societal justice and righteous action."[47]

While the SACEL marked a significant shift in the evangelical position on church-state issues, evangelicals remained reconciliatory rather than confrontational. While noting that "when churches support the politics and philosophy of apartheid the credibility of the gospel is destroyed," they still resolved that resistance should be pursued only through "legitimate channels." If there is any doubt as to what the term "legitimate channels" refers to, it becomes clear later in the same statement when the evangelical leaders called for the withdrawal of military troops from black townships but in the same breath endorsed the presence of the police. "We are concerned that essential law and order be maintained in our communities and we do accept the necessary presence of SAP [South African Police]. We do however urge the immediate withdrawal of the SADF [South African Defence Forces] as their presence has proved to be provocative and inflammatory."[48]

The evangelicals were therefore not ready to question the legitimacy of the state (which is what the SACC was doing) but instead implied that the black uprisings in the townships were a breach of "law and order" and not a legitimate form of political expression by the repressed black population. These church leaders did not question the "law" but instead suggested that it should be upheld. Four years later EFSA produced a document in which it confessed that "Christians [that is, evangelicals] have too often reflected complicity with practices and structures both in church and society which do not reveal scriptural values."[49]

Concerned Evangelicals

In 1985, seven black evangelical leaders, frustrated by EFSA's cautious attitude to apartheid but at the same time alienated by what they saw as the SACC's extreme militancy, formed what came to be known as the Concerned Evangelicals group. Initially led by a black minister in Soweto, Caesar Molebasti,[50] the Concerned Evangelicals attempted to remedy the "theological dualism" characteristic of evangelicals that "permits a separation of faith from politics, the spiritual from the material."[51] The Concerned Evangelicals soon produced a statement titled *Evangelical Witness in South Africa*,[52] calling upon evangelicals to confront the state. The statement challenged evangelicals to "come out boldly [and] take a stand now even if it may mean persecution by earthly systems."[53]

Another evangelical voice critical of the status quo came from an unlikely source: the Pentecostal churches. "A Relevant Pentecostal Witness" was released in 1989 and directly attacked apartheid as the core source of injustice in South Africa. The statement attacked the white supremacy articulated by the Afrikaner churches and established a link between black economic problems and white affluence.[54]

However, these evangelical reactions can rightly be seen as aberrations. In general, evangelicals adopted a middle-of-the-road position on most political issues and were evidently more concerned about the maintenance of doctrinal truth, evangelization, and "Christian unity" than bringing about societal change. For example, after its 1990 general conference, EFSA released a press statement in which it was reported that EFSA members "broke into spontaneous applause" as the Assemblies of God and other evangelical denominations joined the association. There is no mention of the political crisis South Africa was experiencing during this time.[55]

Political Role of Evangelicals

While evangelicals can be criticized for their seeming lack of political concern, they actually played a unique role in South African politics. By taking the middle road, the evangelicals refused to place their full support behind the state, and in a sense distanced themselves from the pro-apartheid Afrikaner churches. Unlike the Afrikaner churches, which were less willing to show remorse for accepting a pro-government position, the evangelicals were often quick to confess that their failure to question apartheid was a betrayal of their Christian calling.

For example, in September 1993, the members of the charismatic group called the International Fellowship of Charismatic Churches (IFCC) came out with a position paper they called "A Christian Manifesto" in which they asked for forgiveness "For our failure, insensitivity and complicity, by neglect of our God-given duty to have addressed the political and social ills of our nation."[56] Such confessions served three purposes. They were directly suggesting that the Afrikaner churches had failed in their God-given duty too; they were directly suggesting that the SACC had actually lived up to its God-given duty; and they were directly stating that there was something seriously wrong with the political system which the IFCC had failed to address. Although this statement came only after the collapse of apartheid, it does reflect a theme present in the evangelical reaction to apartheid from the 1960s onward.

The evangelical churches' mildly critical attitude to the system also placed them in a good position to call for reconciliation among the different church groups. In 1985, Africa Enterprise, an evangelical parachurch group, gathered leaders from both the DRC and the SACC for a conference called the National Initiative of Reconciliation (NIR). The NIR called for the release of all political prisoners, for the acceptance into South Africa of all people in exile, and for talks between the state and opposition groups which would lead to "equitable power sharing in South Africa."[57] Africa Enterprise was able to organize such a gathering in part because it was not perceived as a threat by either the progovernment DRC or the antiapartheid SACC.

After the demise of apartheid in 1990, evangelicals were also in a better position than either the SACC (which was seen as pro-ANC) or the DRC (seen as pro-National Party) to call for reconciliation. In 1993, at the height of the violence in South Africa, Hugh Wetmore condemned the ANC, Inkatha, and the state for creating what he called a "culture of violence."[58] At the same time EFSA held meetings with the ANC, Inkatha, and President De Klerk. EFSA also consulted with the SACC and other church networks. Evangelicals also played a key role in persuading Chief Gatsha Buthelezi to participate in the 1994 elections.[59]

It becomes clear that the mild stand on issues paid some dividends for evangelicals because they could help build goodwill at a time when South Africa was on the brink of civil war. For instance, Michael Cassidy, leader of Africa Enterprise, was able to facilitate reconciliation efforts between the ANC, Inkhatha, and President De Klerk. After meeting with all of them, Cassidy wrote an open letter to Nelson Mandela, President De Klerk, and Chief Buthelezi, trying to show them that they were not as divided as their constituencies made them feel. The letter argued that "In many ways you are closer to each other than you realize. You all talk of a desire to leave the past and to build a new future. You talk of reconciliation, justice, dignity, equality for all. You talk of negotiation leading to peace, economic prosperity and political stability in a non-racial democracy."[60]

Thus the evangelical churches failed to confront the apartheid regime as effectively as the SACC largely because of their concern for Christian unity. However, this placed evangelicals in a better position to call for peace and reconciliation than either the SACC or the DRC. And with the divisive issue of apartheid having been resolved, the evangelical groups discussed above have come together and formed the Evangelical Alliance of South Africa (TEASA), which brings together the Evangelical Fellowship of South Africa, Concerned Evangelicals, and the International Fellowship of Charismatic Churches. One objective of TEASA is to "address from a combined posture and from a biblical point of view various issues in our land relating to church, state and society."[61]

CHURCH-STATE CONFRONTATION: THE SACC MODEL

The DRC played a collaborative role in its dealings with the state during most of the period between 1960 and 1990. To use Bayart's words, they had a "unity of purpose" with the National Party: to serve Afrikaner economic, social, and political interests. The evangelicals on the other hand saw their primary task as being to proclaim and defend the "gospel." A few evangelical groups criticized the state but their influence was limited and in general evangelicals continued to exhibit limited and precautionary involvement in politics. However, after apartheid had been abolished, evangelicals played a more significant role as agents of reconciliation, a role which neither the DRC nor the SACC could play as well because of their previous association with the National Party on the one hand and the ANC on the other.

As will be shown below, it was the SACC which moved into the vacuum created by the banning of black protest movements and took on what Bayart refers to as the "expressly political functions" that brought the SACC into direct confrontation with the state. By the 1970s the SACC had become the "foremost ecumenical agency grouping 'anti-apartheid' churches" and found itself in "continual clashes with the government."[62] The SACC literally assumed the role of the banned African nationalist movements, leading to direct clashes with the state. "For the blacks it is almost the only forum where they can air their aspirations and frustrations."[63] Thus if the DRC-state model represents collaboration, and the evangelical-state model represents limited involvement, the SACC-state model represents confrontation.

Background to the SACC

The irony is that the SACC, like most other Christian groups in South Africa, began essentially as a group designed to serve the interests of the white-dominated Afrikaner churches and the white-led English-speaking churches. The DRC and the other English-speaking denominations established what was then called the General Missionary Conference (GMC) in 1904. The GMC's concerns for the black population were limited to the provision of social services to improve African life and some limited representation of native interests in the law-making processes.

The GMC was reorganized and renamed the Christian Council of South Africa in 1936. The body was composed of twenty-nine churches and missionary groups. But the deep division over race relations and attitudes to state policies led to the breakaway of the DRC from the council in 1939. While the DRC, as noted earlier, moved towards a collaborative role with the state, the council became more critical of the status quo. For example, in 1942 the council held its conference on the campus of the black University of Fort Hare—an unusual practice for white-led organizations in those days. In 1949, the council published a booklet called *Race—What Does the Bible Say?* in which apartheid was criticized for limiting Christian unity to the spiritual realm only.[64]

However, for several decades the council remained a relatively weak organization having only occasional, mild differences with the state. In other words, the council had not taken on the political function of representing black aspirations. These were adequately represented by the ANC, the Pan African Congress (PAC), and other black movements in society. However, by the 1960s the white minority government had deactivated all elements of civil society that were perceived as a threat to the status quo. Having disenfranchised the black majority and weakened the white liberal opposition in parliament, the National Party ushered in an airtight era in South African politics. Mandela, speaking at his trial, expressed black frustration at the stifling of black political activity: "All lawful modes of expressing opposition to this principle [of white supremacy] had been closed by legislation, and we were placed in a position in which we had either to accept a permanent state of inferiority,

or to defy the Government. We chose to defy the Government. We chose
to defy the law."[65]

In 1963 Mandela was sentenced to life imprisonment. But there was
no respite in the state's onslaught against black political movements.
Black leaders either were banned or fled into exile. It was virtually impossible to organize mass political activity because of the increased
members of state informants planted in the black community. By the mid
1960s therefore it could be said that the state had effectively "crippled
black political resistance to apartheid."[66]

Filling the Vacuum

It was this vacuum that eventually pushed the South African Council
of Churches into direct political confrontation with the state. The
churches were one element of civil society that the state could not repress
as it had repressed other nationalist groups. The irony is that this was
because the National Party itself was composed of Christian people who
had a deep respect for religion. The National Party constituency had no
respect for liberation movements, but had a lot of respect for churches—
even black churches. The state therefore had to be careful not to appear
to be persecuting Christians because in South Africa, as in all of Africa,
religion enjoys a certain amount of legitimacy in society and therefore
the state invariably hesitates to directly repress the churches.

In South Africa, the only way the government could justify any attempts to silence the churches was by persuading its Christian constituency that the SACC had been infiltrated by nationalists and communists,
who were using the churches as a bastion for their antigovernment activities. For example, in the mid 1970s, the state funded a Christian
League of South Africa which repeatedly accused the SACC of having
strayed from the "gospel." The league claimed that the SACC had become an instrument of communism and nationalism. When it became
known that the league was funded by the state's Information Department,
the government was embarrassed.[67]

The churches, however, did not quickly jump into the vacuum that
was created in the 1960s. One reason for this was that the SACC was
still led by white South Africans who, despite their opposition to apartheid, did not feel the urgency for change that blacks felt. Therefore, the
SACC's behavior in the 1960s, though threatening to the state, was not
as directly confrontational as it was to become in later years. The
SACC's key role in the 1960s, when apartheid seemed to have become

entrenched, was to continue making and publishing disturbing commentaries about the political system.

In 1965 the council hosted a conference which concluded that "it is often necessary and important that Christians of different races should be able to live under one roof and share a common board."[68] The council then requested special permission to put this idea into practice by holding a mixed-residence conference. Prime Minister Verwoerd responded: "Your churches should be able to fulfill their functions fully as other Protestants [*sic*] churches do while observing the country's laws and customs as they exist."[69] In other words, Verwoerd was saying to the SACC that if its primary concern was Christian ministry like "other Protestants" (meaning the DRC) then it need not raise questions of racial integration or call for changes in the status quo. And if the SACC continued to do so, then the implication would be that it was committed to other functions—in Bayart's words—to "distinctly political functions."

In 1968, the SACC published a document called a "Message to the People of South Africa" in which it declared that apartheid contradicted the principles of the Christian faith and therefore that Christianity obliged believers to go against the laws of the South African state. Coming at a time when the state thought it had effectively quelled any opposition to apartheid, but also at a time when the church-based civil rights movement in America was making gains, the statement both alarmed and infuriated state officials.

The reaction of Prime Minister Vorster to the above statement reveals the fear that a church-based antiapartheid movement could emerge and make the same gains that the civil rights movement was making in America.[70] Vorster told the SACC that his government would not permit them to "do the kind of thing here in South Africa that Martin Luther King did in America." And revealing his concern about the potential influence of the churches, Vorster told the SACC to "cut it out, cut it out immediately, for the cloak you carry will not protect you if you try to do this in South Africa."[71]

The fact that the SACC was a member of the often radical World Council of Churches (WCC) frequently provided the state with good reason to attack the SACC as a front for an international communist agenda. This came to a climax in 1969 when the WCC held a conference on racism and seemed to conclude that armed activity against a racist state was justifiable if no means of peaceful negotiation was possible. In other words the WCC was endorsing the decision made by the ANC in the early 1960s to form Umkotho we Sizwe.

The WCC created what was called the Program to Combat Racism (PCR), which in 1970 offered financial aid to humanitarian programs of the ANC and other liberation movements in Southern Africa. The news that the SACC's mother body had granted funds to the banned ANC provided fuel for the state's position that the SACC was a front for the banned antigovernment organizations. The SACC refused to budge, although it distanced itself from specific financial grants made to the ANC.

Two questions arise from this conflict over WCC's support for the ANC. First of all, why did the state not ban the SACC since it had ample proof that the SACC sympathized with the exiled ANC? Second, why did the SACC not withdraw from the WCC since WCC activities were increasing church-state hostility in South Africa?

The answer to the first question is central to the overall explanation of the role of churches in African politics. The answer is that the African state is not strong enough to directly repress the churches, in part because religion enjoys a privileged status and greater legitimacy than the state itself. Therefore, although state officials could threaten SACC clergy (and occasionally harass them) and although the action of the WCC could have provided enough information to ban the SACC, the decision to directly clamp down on the churches was never made. For example, the Christian Institute and the Black Consciousness Movement (BCM), both closely related to the SACC, were banned in 1977 but SACC survived, and with the rise of Desmond Tutu as its first black leader, the SACC maintained its political fervency until 1990. The state refused to quell the SACC.

The rise of Tutu to the position of general secretary of the SACC helps to explain why the SACC never left the WCC: the SACC's leadership and membership had by now become black. How this came about is best explained by examining some of the changes that took place in the South African Christian community in the late 1960s.

The SACC Becomes Black

As noted, the SACC began as a loose ecumenical body of mostly black, but white-controlled, churches. Early in the 1960s this began to change. Missionary organizations, partially in response to pressure from their black membership and partially due to dwindling resources, began to pull out and let the now mature black churches assume more autonomy. For example, the Lutheran churches, though "numerically strong," had not taken any significant part in South African politics because they were "under the control of conservative missionaries." But once the missionaries withdrew, many churches of the Lutheran tradition joined the SACC. The "blackening" of the SACC was completed by the early 1970s as the indigenous African Independence Churches Association joined the SACC in 1971 and the black "daughter" churches of the DRC assumed an observer status.[72]

The SACC became black not only in its membership but also in its leadership. In 1971, August Habegraan, a Lutheran minister, became the first black president of the ecumenical body. In 1978, Desmond Tutu, a black Anglican minister, became the general secretary. He was to lead the SACC through its most violent confrontation with the state.[73]

The Christian Institute and the Black Consciousness Movement

While the changes in the membership and leadership of the SACC were significant factors in determining the political functions of its member churches, the primary factors still lay in the state of civil society. While there were other elements of civil society that could have exercised these functions, the churches tended to shy away from direct confrontation, in part because these functions were being exercised by other groups. This is clearly the case here. When the state banned black movements in 1960, other institutions emerged that were church-based but were still outside direct church jurisdiction.

The first such institution was the Christian Institute founded by Beyers Naude, a renegade DRC minister, in 1963.[74] The Christian Institute was founded during the crisis following the 1960 Sharpeville killings and the declaration of a state of emergency. The state of emergency enabled the government to clamp down, at least temporarily, on black political activism, and the Christian Institute emerged to play a role in informing the world of the evils of apartheid.[75] "It was the Christian Institute that became a thoroughly disturbing prophetic voice: describing the full impact of apartheid on blacks, condemning the structures of injustice, assailing complacency, struggling to articulate an alternative vision for society and trying to discern appropriate methods to bring something of that vision into being."[76]

The Christian Institute provided direction and leadership for antiracist activities. According to De Gruchy, it was "in the forefront of Christian resistance to apartheid."[77] While the Christian Institute was active the SACC felt relatively unpressured because the institute "took on . . . the many responsibilities that the Council might have assumed."[78] Furthermore, the SACC cooperated on many projects with the Christian Institute, leading to the publication of critical statements about the state.[79] The Christian Institute also became a forum for the Black Consciousness Movement[80] led by Steve Biko.[81] The BCM advocated a "black" theology which was threatening to the white establishment.[82]

By the late 1970s, the Christian Institute and the Black Consciousness Movement had also become victims of state oppression. Biko was arrested several times and finally died in detention on 12 September 1977. Other leaders of the BCM were also arrested during early morning raids by police. On 17 October 1977, the Christian Institute was banned and so were all its leaders. The state also banned several related newspapers and arrested their journalists and editors.

The vacuum that had appeared briefly in the early 1960s, following the arrest of black leaders and the banning of the ANC and the PAC, reappeared. "The annihilation of black political organizations in 1960 had been repeated seventeen years later."[83] Again the state seemed to have triumphed over civil society. As Gatsha Buthelezi put it, the move by the state was a "politically ruthless action" that had taken away the "only reason" for hope in the black population. The SACC declared 17 October "a terrible day for South Africa."[84]

The experience of the Christian Institute and the Black Consciousness Movement illuminates some valuable points about the viability of para-church groups—organizations that derive their existence from the churches but are autonomous—as actors in African politics. The first is that such groups are able to engage the state more aggressively because they attract people of like mind and are therefore monolithic. The churches, because of their pastoral role, try to be as accommodating as possible and this leads to ambiguity in church-state relations. The second point illuminated by this experience is that the state can more easily clamp down on para-church groups than on the churches themselves. It was easier for the South Africa government to ban the Christian Institute than it would have been to ban, say, the Anglican Church. It was also easier to clamp down on Steve Biko's BCM than it would have been to ban a whole denomination that espoused black theology. The monolithic nature of para-church organizations therefore is a strength in that it provides a basis for aggressive action, but it is also a weakness in that it provides an oppressive state with the opportunity to isolate these groups and penalize them with relatively little political risk. In this case, therefore, we see that while the banning of the Christian Institute and the BCM provoked some reaction, the state emerged apparently victorious.

As will be shown below, when the SACC took over these functions and began to confront the state directly, one source of security the SACC had was its ecclesiastical authority. For example, in 1979, Prisons Minister Louis Le Grange claimed that the SACC had communist connections—a claim which in other cases could have led to banning. Tutu reminded the state that the SACC was a "Council of Churches, not a private organization." He added: "If they take the SACC and the churches on, let them just know they are taking on the Church of Jesus Christ."[85]

In a secular society such rhetoric may not have as much effect. But Tutu knew that the Afrikaner officials were religious people and the idea of victimizing the church, even if it included black people, was discomforting. In other words, while the South African state could clamp down on other groups in civil society, it could not with a free conscience do the same to the SACC. Hence after 1977, the SACC emerged as the foremost critic of the state and remained so until 1990 when apartheid was abandoned.

THE SACC CONFRONTS THE STATE

In 1978 when Tutu assumed leadership of the South African Council of Churches, the critical question was whether the SACC would fill the vacuum created by the banning of the Christian Institute and BCM. It did not take long to see that this was the direction the SACC would take. Unlike the evangelicals, who were guarded in their attack on apartheid, the SACC spoke the language of the banned ANC. "I want to declare categorically that I believe apartheid to be evil and immoral, and therefore unchristian," said Tutu, who epitomized the SACC response to apartheid during this era.[86]

At its 1978 conference, the SACC called upon the international investor community not to invest in industries and business enterprises that perpetuated apartheid policies. In 1979, the SACC's conference theme, "The Church and the Alternative Society," was even more provocative, with guest speaker Jesse Jackson declaring that South African blacks were in slavery. It was at this conference that the SACC began to directly question the legitimacy of the South African government. The SACC members agreed not to cooperate with the state if the state's law "violated the justice of God."[87]

The SACC therefore provided a blessing, a forum, and a voice to individuals and groups that formed the antiapartheid movement. In Tutu's words, "We are challenged by our Lord's example to work for those in prison, the poor and oppressed, the homeless and despised."[88]

SACC set up what it called a Dependents' Conference—a unit that provided legal, emotional, and economic support to the families of those who had been arrested by the state. In 1979, at least seven hundred families were beneficiaries of this program. The SACC helped fund the funeral expenses of victims of violence; the same fund paid the legal fees for those accused by the state of participating in antigovernment activities. In other words, the SACC offered its resources to the very elements of society the state was geared to eliminate; it supported the illegal political opposition.

Rhetorical Activity

Another powerful way in which SACC confronted the state was through rhetorical activity. The SACC and its member churches used church services, mass funerals, and other religious gatherings to criticize the state. Since these were expressly religious gatherings it was difficult for the state to restrict them. For example, at the funeral service and memorial services for Steve Biko, the banned Black Consciousness leader, Tutu, then bishop of Lesotho, described Biko as a prophet called by God to confront the evil governmental system: "God called Steve Biko to be his servant in South Africa—to speak up on behalf of God, declaring what the will of this God must be in a situation such as ours, a situation of evil, injustice, oppression and exploitation."[89]

This is a stronger endorsement of Biko's politics than any legal secular organization would have dared to give. With regard to the government minister of police, who had made some cold remarks about Biko's death, Tutu declared: "Of all human beings, he is to be the most pitied." The speech concludes with Tutu appealing to the gathered masses to commit themselves to "the struggle for the liberation of our beloved land, South Africa."[90]

The SACC reacted similarly to the death of Robert Mangaliso Sobukwe, founder of the radical Pan Africanist Congress (PAC). Sobukwe was detained on Robben Island for six years, and upon his release, banned from public activity. He died in 1978. Speaking at his memorial service, Tutu again painted a different picture of Sobukwe from that painted by the state, which portrayed him as radical, violent, and a Godless communist. Tutu said: "He was a holy man, devoted to Jesus Christ his Lord and Master, and for that reason committed to seeing radical change happening in South Africa without violence and bloodshed, death and destruction." Tutu then turned around and criticized the state for refusing to talk to leaders of the banned black movements such as the ANC and PAC. "The tragedy of this country is that the powers that be have consistently refused to parley with such as Robert."[91]

The rhetorical activity of the clergy quite often became theatrical. For instance, Tutu, knowing full well that the police would not permit it, visited Winnie Mandela with the intention of celebrating Holy Communion with her. The police did not permit him to enter her house. Tutu and Winnie Mandela celebrated Communion in Tutu's car. On another day they had Communion on Winnie Mandela's fence since Tutu was not permitted on her property: "This time Winnie was on one side of the fence and I on the other."[92] The effect of such public activity in the black township of Soweto cannot be underestimated. Again it must be noted that while a clergyman could ridicule state restrictions in this way, others would have been arrested by the state and imprisoned or banned.

What these examples indicate is that churches and religious gatherings become fora for expounding the beliefs and ideas of banned groups, and for publicly praising banned black leaders. Such rhetorical activity was only possible in the churches and from church leaders. The churches offered the rhetorical power of their leaders as a resource to further the interests of banned groups in civil society and to embarrass the state.[93]

Delegitimizing the State: The 1980s

The 1980s ushered in the most oppressive time in South African history. Troops of the South African Defence Forces (SADF) moved into black townships. By 1984 there were an estimated seven thousand soldiers deployed in the streets, shooting up to thirty-five thousand people in 1985. The South African Police (SAP) doubled its manpower from 1984 to 1987 and its primary role was to fight black opposition. Over twenty-nine thousand people were in detention by 1986.[94]

In 1985 a group of theologians produced what came to be known as the "Kairos Document,"[95] which sharply criticized the DRC's "state theology" as "the theological justification of the status quo with its racism, capitalism and totalitarianism."[96] The Kairos Document also criticized some churches as being "limited, guarded and cautious" in their stand against the state. The Kairos statement called for a "prophetic theology" which is "always confrontational." Such a theology "confronts the evils of the time and speaks out against them in no uncertain terms."[97]

Although the SACC member churches did not accept the Kairos Document in its totality, its influence on church-state relations was indisputable. An ecumenical conference of churches held in Zimbabwe in 1985 endorsed the Kairos position and declared the liberation struggle just and the South African state unjust.[98]

Therefore, from the mid 1980s many SACC member churches adopted the position that the South African state was illegitimate and therefore did not deserve the support of the churches. In 1984 the SACC adopted a resolution calling upon the churches to pray for the end of unjust rule.[99] Although this resolution caused some controversy and did not rally as much support as had been hoped it did indicate that the SACC wanted the apartheid regime to go. At the 1987 conference in Lusaka, the SACC publicly declared that the South African state was illegitimate. Two years later, the SACC, joined by the Southern African Catholic Bishops' Conference, reiterated its position. The SACC clearly placed itself in direct confrontation with the state.[100]

Legitimizing Antiapartheid Movements

Having declared the apartheid regime illegitimate, the churches now openly endorsed the banned ANC and other antiapartheid organizations as the source for the creation of a legitimate government for South Africa. In other words, the churches had stepped in to fill the vacuum by mobilizing support and maintaining pressure on the state at a time when most black movements were banned. But the church leaders realized that their political function had limits: they could not offer people the promise of an alternative government. It was therefore necessary that these banned and exiled movements reemerge inside South Africa and begin to mobilize the black constituency in order to achieve real political power.

Following its banning and the arrest of its leaders in the 1960s, the ANC established its headquarters in Zambia and basically became a movement in exile. Therefore, from 1960 to 1978, most of the antiapartheid activity in South Africa arose as a result of spontaneous uprisings in townships, but there was no nationally organized movement of the stature of the ANC. The SACC become more involved in politics largely because of the vacuum created by the deactivation of the ANC and other nationalist movements. During most of this period, the churches (together with a number of often short-lived movements) were challenging apartheid from the inside while the ANC was hoping to bring down the establishment through internationalized, largely Soviet-backed guerilla warfare.[101]

In 1978, the ANC realized that this approach was faulty and decided to reenter South Africa and begin to press for change from within.[102] The new strategy was to bring about change, not through guerilla warfare, but through political organizations within South Africa. Thanks to the churches and other movements that had kept up the pressure, the state was actually losing ground and the ANC began to see the possibility of a peaceful victory. The ANC then established what it called the Internal Reconstruction and Development Department, which was to operate underground inside South Africa. Its objective was to mobilize the activated civil society into a power base for the ANC. That church leaders were part of this change in the ANC strategy is not easy to verify, but it is evident that many of them kept contact with the ANC leaders in exile. In the 1980s, church leaders met openly with ANC leaders in Zambia and Zimbabwe.[103]

Quite evidently therefore, the churches realized that the political functions they had assumed were temporary and that there was a need for the ANC to reemerge and provide leadership to the black population. The United Democratic Front (UDF) was formed in 1983 and temporarily served as the internal wing of the ANC. Its influence, however, was limited to the mostly Coloured and Indian groups who had limited sympathy for the black majority.[104] Although the UDF claimed responsibility for mass protests in the black townships, there is evidence that most of these were spontaneous and the UDF, in the words of one of its leaders, was "trailing behind the masses." For example, the minutes of one UDF meeting reveal that "The masses expected UDF to give direction, [but] the UDF was not there to give direction."[105]

The UDF was banned in 1988 but civil society had been so activated that it could not be repressed as it had been in 1960. The SACC, later led by Frank Chikane, continued to serve as the bastion of the mass democratic movement, living up to its reputation as the "ANC at prayer."

In December 1989 the National Party, led by the relatively liberal De Klerk, finally responded to the call to dismantle apartheid. In an implied acknowledgment of the power of the churches, De Klerk appealed to the churches to "formulate a strategy conducive to negotiation, reconciliation and change."[106] On 2 February 1990, De Klerk announced plans to dismantle apartheid and, on 11 February, he released Nelson Mandela from prison. Tutu later attributed De Klerk's change of heart to divine intervention. "He [God] worked to inspire the state president to act in an unexpectedly courageous manner."[107]

The End of Church-State Confrontation

After the release of the black leaders and the unbanning of the nationalist movements, the SACC stepped out of the limelight. "An immediate consequence was that church leaders who had been at the forefront of the struggle became less prominent. Some, like Archbishop Tutu, were the first to recognize that they were no longer the political representatives of the oppressed. Frank Chikane, who had taken over leadership of the SACC from Tutu, also left his position in 1994 because the victory over apartheid was now a "mission accomplished."[108]

The response of the churches to the liberation of civil society supports the theoretical propositions advanced in the first chapter of this book. Now that the vacuum that had sucked the churches into direct confrontation with the state had been filled by the reactivation of the ANC, the churches no longer needed to perform the political functions that they had gradually assumed since the banning of the ANC and the arrest of its leaders in the 1960s.

CHURCHES AFTER APARTHEID

In November 1991, 230 church leaders representing eighty denominations and forty para-church groups met in Rustenburg to determine the role of the churches in postapartheid South Africa. The conference was unique because, for the first time since 1960, the DRC was participating in a conference together with other churches. At the same conference, a respected DRC minister, Willie Jonker, confessed that he and the DRC were guilty of supporting the apartheid regime.

Tutu was quick to accept the apology, stating that he was responding to the pressure of the Holy Spirit to say "I forgive you."[109] But Tutu's forgiving spirit was not welcomed by all and they made this known to him. At a later session of this conference Tutu said it had come to his attention that some had observed that he had no authority to accept the DRC apology for anyone "other than myself" and admitted that it was "rather presumptuous of me to suggest that I was speaking on behalf of anybody."[110]

Other church leaders wanted the DRC to organize a special forum at which it would express repentance. For example, Beyers Naude, the DRC minister who was ejected from the denomination in 1963 and became leader of the antiapartheid Christian Institute, called upon the DRC to apologize to the whole black community "because it—more than any other—was responsible for asking for specific laws and actions in order to promote and strengthen the policy of apartheid." Naude said the DRC should organize a gathering on the banks of the Blood River or some similar place and make a public confession of guilt. He also challenged the DRC to apologize to the international Christian community, particularly the WCC.[111]

Although the Rustenburg conference was supposed to mark the beginning of a new era, it seems to have marked the end of one. With apartheid out of the way, it was clear that church-state relations in South Africa would no longer be confrontational. Compared to earlier statements, *The Rustenburg Declaration* is disappointing.[112] The section on church-state relations comprises a few paragraphs calling for the adoption of democratic processes of governance. Since both the government and the opposition groups were calling for the same actions, the Rustenburg Declaration seems to lack any new insights. The voice of the churches was now drowned by the many voices of activated civil society.

However, the abrupt departure of the churches from their position as a key political influence only heightens their importance in the history of the antiapartheid movement. De Gruchy speaks for most students of church-state relations in South Africa when he concludes: "Although the witness of the church was sometimes sullied by compromise, and while there were other important players, there can be little doubt that the church played a key role in the ending of apartheid."[113]

The challenge of the churches today is to define a role in the new South Africa. A pessimistic view is that they will be "confined to being an ignored and peripheral force."[114] Another possibility is that they will complement the state in its economic development program.[115] In the concluding chapter of this book, a new role for churches in pluralist Africa is proposed.

CONCLUSION

The above analysis of the evolution of church-state relations in South Africa supports the contention that the repression of civil society is the primary explanation for the activation of churches into political activity.

The white South African state, in its attempt to control black protest organizations, banned the ANC and other nationalist groups in the 1960s. Leaders of these organizations were arrested or fled into exile. The churches emerged as the only element of civil society with the potential to make an autonomous impact on state policy. The rise of Desmond Tutu and other black clergymen in the SACC, and the prevailing repression of other groups, soon elevated the SACC into the main opposition organization to the state. The SACC's role became what Bayart would call that of a "zone of liberty" eventually leading to the activation of other civil society groups which culminated in the formation of mass democratic organizations in the late 1980s.

It was the pressure of these nationwide movements, in many cases still led by members of the clergy and still meeting in church buildings and compounds, that led to the end of apartheid in 1990. But the end of apartheid marked a significant drop in the role of the churches in politics. This was manifested by the 1990 Rustenburg Declaration which, compared to the earlier antiapartheid statements, showed that the churches had lost their power. The best they could now do was to make lengthy appeals to the real actors—the newly liberated civil society organizations.

NOTES

1. See Paul Maylam, *A History of the African People of South Africa: From the Early Iron Age to the 1970s* (New York: St Martin's Press, 1986).

2. Marjorie Hope and James Young. *The South African Churches in a Revolutionary Situation* (New York: Orbis Books, 1981), 11.

3. Peter Hinchcliff, *The Church in South Africa* (London: SPCK, 1968), 10.

4. For a history of the Catholic Church, see William Eric Brown, *The Catholic Church in South Africa: From Its Origins to the Present Day* (London: Burns and Oates, 1960). See also Garth Abraham, *The Catholic Church and Apartheid: The Response of the Catholic Church in South Africa to the First Decade of the National Party Rule 1948–1957* (Johannesburg: Ravan Press, 1989).

5. Charles Villa-Vicencio, *Trapped in Apartheid: A Socio-Theological History of the English-Speaking Churches* (New York: Orbis Books, 1988), 16.

6. Andre Odendaal, *Black Protest Politics in South Africa to 1912* (Totowa, NJ: Barnes and Noble Books, 1984), 3.

7. Ibid., 24.

8. H.P.P. Lotter, "Religion and Politics in Transforming South Africa," *Journal of Church and State* 34, 3 (Summer 1992): 475.

9. Peter Walshe, *Church versus State in South Africa: The Case of the Christian Institute* (New York: Orbis Books, 1983), 66–69.

10. For example, Villa-Vicencio argues that these churches have a more "definite separation between spiritual values and socio-political reality [and] it is this as much as anything else that has prevented these churches from developing into the kinds of movements" that could confront the state. See *Trapped in Apartheid*, 35.

11. Linda E. Thomas, "African Indigenous Churches as a Source of Socio-Political Transformation in South Africa," *Africa Today* 41 (1994): 39–56.

12. For studies of the role of some of the major SACC member denominations in South African politics, see Desmond Van Der Water, "Born out of Unity and for Unity: The Witness of the United Congregational Church of Southern Africa in South Africa," 159–162; Nancy Charton, "The Witness of the Church of the Province of Southern Africa," pp. 153–157; and Daryl Balia, "The Witness of the Methodist Church in South Africa," 163–165. All these articles appeared in *International Review of Mission* (1 January 1994).

13. Villa-Vicencio, *Trapped in Apartheid*, 45.

14. Willem Saayem, in *Christianity amidst Apartheid*, ed. Martin Prozesky (New York: St. Martin's Press, 1990) 30.

15. Albert Luthuli, "Africa and Freedom," in *Africa's Freedom* (London: Unwin Books, 1964), 7.

16. Lotter, 477.

17. Patrick Johnstone, *Operation World: The Day by Day Guide to Praying for the World* (Grand Rapids, MI: Zondervan Publishing House, 1993), 494.

18. See "The Roman Catholics," in Hope and Young, 154–168.

19. Johnstone, 494.

20. Hope and Young, 123–153.

21. Louw Alberts and Frank Chikane, eds., *The Road to Rustenberg: The Church Looking forward to a New South Africa* (Cape Town: Struik, 1991), 78.

22. Johnstone, 495.

23. Villa-Vicencio, *Trapped in Apartheid*, 23.

24. Johann Kinghorn, "The Theology of Separate Equality: A Critical Outline of the DRC's Position on Apartheid," in *Christianity amidst Apartheid*, ed. Martin Prozesky (New York: St. Martin's Press, 1990), 57–80.

25. Ibid., 58.

26. Ibid., 58.

27. Ibid., 58.

28. Ibid., 61.

29. Ibid., 62.

30. Alex Laguma, *Apartheid* (New York: International Publishers, 1971), 24.

31. Ibid., 67.

32. Jean-François Bayart, "La Fonction Politique des Eglises au Cameroon," *Revve Francaise de Science Politique* 3 (3 June 1973), 514.

33. Hope and Young, 1–2.

34. Villa-Vicencio, *Trapped in Apartheid*, 23.

35. Lotter, 487.

36. As quoted by Kinghorn, 47.

37. Lotter, 482.

38. Villa-Vicencio, *Trapped in Apartheid*, 24.

39. Johnstone, 94.

40. For example, there is no chapter on evangelicals in Hope and Young, *The Churches in a Revolutionary Situation*.

41. Villa-Vicencio, *Trapped in Apartheid*, 39.

42. Ibid., 40.

43. By "body" theology I mean the Pauline teaching that Christians all belong to the body of Christ despite their racial and other differences.

44. *Evangelense* 3 (1995), 4.

45. Ibid.

46. "A Charter for Mobilizing Evangelical Unity," produced by the South African Conference of Evangelical Leaders, sponsored by the Evangelical Fellowship of South Africa (1985), 1.

47. Ibid., 13.

48. Ibid., 14–15.

49. *Understanding South Africa: A Study Guide to Help Christians Understand the Social Dynamic from an Evangelical Perspective* (Pietermaritzburg: Evangelical Fellowship of South Africa, 1989), 24.

50. For a profile, see Caesar Molebatsi with David Virtue, *A Flame for Justice: The Man Whose Heart Burns for the Youth of Soweto—The Citizens of South Africa's Tomorrow* (London: Lion Publishing, 1991).

51. *Evangelens* 3 (1995), 2.

52. Concerned Evangelicals, *Evangelical Witness in South Africa* (Grand Rapids, MI: Eerdmans, 1986).

53. Molebatsi and Virtue, 137.

54. Lotter, 483–484.

55. "The EFSA 1990 AGM: Evangelical Unity Is Growing" (News Release, 26 March 1990).

56. Neville Woudberg, "Michael Cassidy Letter Appeals for Reconciliation," *World Evangelical Report* (15 October 1993).

57. John de Gruchy, *Christianity and Democracy: A Theology for a Just World Order* (New York: Cambridge University Press, 1995), 208.

58. Isaac Phiri, "We Have Been Creating a Culture of Violence," *World Evangelical Report* (15 February 1993), 12–13.

59. See Val Waldeck, "The Day God Saved South Africa," *Christian Reader* (March/April, 1996), 82–89.

60. Woudberg.

61. *Afroscope* (May 1995), 10.

62. Hope and Young, 86.

63. Ibid., 86.

64. John De Gruchy, *The Church Struggle in South Africa* (Grand Rapids, MI: Eerdman's 1979), 53.

65. Walshe, *Church versus State*, 44.

66. Ibid., 43.

67. See Desmond Tutu, *Crying in the Wilderness* (London: Mowbray, 1986), 28.

68. *Christian Council Quarterly*, (Fourth Quarter, 1965): 2.

69. Ibid., 7.

70. For a comparative study of the South African protest movements and the American civil rights experience, see George M. Fredrickson, *Black Liberation: A Comparative History of Black Ideologies in the United States and South Africa* (New York: Oxford University Press, 1995).

71. Hope and Young, 89.

72. Ibid., 88.

73. For a profile, see Shirley Du Boulay, *Tutu: Voice of the Voiceless* (Grand Rapids, MI: Eerdman's, 1988).

74. Walshe, *Church versus State*.

75. See also Peter Walshe, "The Christian Institute and African Nationalism," *Journal of Church and State* (Autumn 1977): 460.

76. Walshe, *Church versus State*, 42.

77. De Gruchy, *Christianity and Democracy*, 206.

78. Hope and Young, 87.

79. For example, the Study Project on Christianity in Apartheid. See Hope and Young, 102–127.

80. See Robert Fatton Jr., *Black Consciousness in South Africa* (New York: State University of New York Press, 1986).

81. Donald Woods, *Biko* (New York: Vintage Books, 1979).

82. See Takatso Mofokeng, "Black Theology in South Africa: Achievements, Problems and Prospects," in *Christianity amidst Apartheid*, ed. Martin Prozesk (New York: St Martin's Press, 1990), 37–53.

83. Walshe, *Church versus State*, 222.

84. Ibid.

85. Tutu, *Crying in the Wilderness*, 31.

86. Ibid., 29.

87. *Ecunews* (3 August 1979).

88. Tutu, *Crying in the Wilderness*, 25.

89. Ibid., 44–47.

90. Ibid.

91. Ibid., 48–49.

92. Ibid., 52.

93. For a collection of Tutu's speeches, see Naomi Tutu, *The Words of Desmond Tutu: Selected by Naomi Tutu* (New York: Newmarket Press, 1989).

94. Borer, "Challenging the State: Churches as Political Actors in South Africa," *Journal of Church and State* 35, 2 (Spring 1993): 316.

95. For a complete statement, see "The Kairos Document: A Theological Comment on the Political Crisis in South Africa," in Robert McAfee Brown, *Kairos: Three Prophetic Challenges to the Church* (Grand Rapids, MI: Eerdmans, 1990).

96. Ibid., 29.

97. Ibid., 49.

98. De Gruchy, *Christianity and Democracy*, 210.

99. See Allan A. Boesak and Charles Villa-Vicencio, eds., *When Prayer Makes News* (Philadelphia: Westminster Press, 1986).

100. Borer, 299.

101. See "Soviet Strategy toward the ANC," in Daniel Kempton, *Soviet Strategy toward African National Liberation Movements* (New York: Praeger, 1989).

102. Howard Barrel, " 'The Turn to the Masses': The African National Congress Strategic Review of 1978–79," *Journal of Southern African Studies* 18, 1 (March 1992).

103. De Gruchy, *Christianity and Democracy*, 210.

104. Jeremy Seekings, "Trailing behind Masses: The United Democratic Front and Township Politics in the Pretoria-Witersrand-Vaal Region, 1983–84," *Journal of Southern African Studies* 18, 1 (March 1992).

105. Ibid., 106.

106. Louw Alberts and Frank Chikane, *The Road to Rustenberg: The Church Looking forward to a New South Africa* (Cape Town: Struik, 1991), 14.

107. Ibid., 20.

108. See "Chikane to Leave Council of Churches," in *Christian Century* (27 July–3 August 1994), 717.

109. Ibid., 99.

110. Ibid., 100.

111. Ibid., 227.

112. Louw Alberts and Frank Chikane, eds. *The Rustenburg Declaration: The Church Looking Forward to a New South Africa* (Cape Town: Struik, 1991).

113. De Grunchy, *Christianity and Democracy*, 211.

114. John M. Lamola, "Change Is Pain: A Projective Reflection on the Mission of the Church in South Africa beyond 1994," *International Review of Mission* (January 1994).

115. See Klaus Nurnberger, "The Task of the Church Concerning the Economy in a Post-apartheid South Africa," *Missionalia* 22, 2 (August 1994): 118–146.

Proclaiming Politics of Peace and Love: A New Role for Churches in Pluralist Africa

Guy Hermet observed that in political systems characterized by "authoritarian exercise of power and . . . refusal to implement a sufficient and generalized participation of the citizen in the political system . . . religious organizations are the only ones capable of offering host structures, leadership, and means of expression distinct from those controlled by the power dominating oligarchy."[1] This has been the case in sub-Saharan Africa in the last four decades. As governance degenerated into authoritarian rule, churches emerged as, in most cases, the only formidable opposition to the state. Therefore, churches became one significant factor in the ending of apartheid in South Africa and the demise of other forms of repressive governance in the rest of Africa.

Thus, the 1990s—thanks in part to the role of the churches—have been a decade of transition from state hegemony to political pluralism. But the adoption of multiparty constitutions and related democratic procedures has introduced new challenges to African society. Some countries, such as Kenya, which were relatively tranquil during the one-party period have, in recent times, become more volatile. In other cases, there have been violent reversals of democratic gains made earlier. In Sierra Leone the newly elected government of Ahmad Tejan Kabbah had to be restored by force after it was overthrown by the disgruntled military.[2] Therefore, while Africans have cause for optimism, the continent is still a long way from eliminating conflict. In other words, lasting peace—the removal of violence from political conduct—still eludes Africa.

The questions this chapter seeks to address are the following: What is the role of the churches in pluralist Africa? Does the ending of repressive regimes and the emergence of many civil society organizations completely extinguish the role of organized Christianity in Africa? Is there a unique contribution that churches in Africa can bring to the fostering of peace as their societies experiment with multiparty politics? By way of responding to these questions, this chapter will (1) review the role churches played in the transitions to pluralism not just in Zambia, Zimbabwe, and South Africa but in other cases as well; (2) point out some of the new threats to peace that democratization has introduced; (3) advance and substantiate the thesis that the most valuable contribution churches can make toward peaceful politics in pluralist Africa is to introduce and infuse selfless love of other humans as a guiding ethic in the practice of competitive politics; and (4) propose some ways in which this can be done.

At first, such a proposition appears to be too idealistic and devoid of any pragmatic value. Yet, such an assumption is misleading for two reasons. First, the involvement of the churches in Africa is often motivated by idealism. Desmond Tutu and the South African Council of Churches, for example, were motivated by idealistic opposition to apartheid. An idealistic commitment to the creation of a socially just society has powerful and pragmatic implications. Second, the transition to political pluralism—though in and of itself a desirable change—has taken place in environments that are hostile to the flourishing of pluralistic democracy. In most of Africa, there are no strong democratic institutions, few means to administer and police democratic procedures, and no established ways to deal with grievances. Therefore, unless political leaders and their followers are restrained by a strong ethical commitment to selfless love of political opponents, competitive politics will most likely foster violent intrastate conflict which may easily cross national borders and become international.

This chapter argues that the new role of the churches in pluralist Africa is to infuse the individual members of the societies in which they operate with the ideals of the Golden Rule and to challenge the political elite with the same message. The contention is that churches must resist being made irrelevant by the political parties and other movements that have mushroomed in pluralist Africa, and instead, focus their resources on teaching and challenging the members and leaders of these organizations to integrate Christ's Law of Love into their political practice. The power of selfless love in conflict resolution and peacemaking begs for more attention in peace research. M. Darrol Bryant has observed that love is "the transforming ground of our life together" and that the call to love other humans is "profoundly simple, yet the most difficult of achievements."[3] Richard L. Johnson and Eric Ledbetter explored the impact of Christ's Law of Love on the political activism of Gandhi.[4] Martin Luther King Jr. is quoted as saying, "Love for Gandhi was a potent instrument for social and collective transformation."[5] This chapter advances this line of thinking, applying it specifically to the African context. It argues that Christ's teaching about love is critical to conflict resolution and peace-making in Africa's fragile transitions to pluralist democracies. It calls upon churches to bring the power of Christ's Law of Love to bear upon the political life of Africa.

ROLE OF CHURCHES IN TRANSITIONS TO PLURALISM

The optimism that greeted the end of colonial rule in most of Africa in the late 1950s and early 1960s soon disappeared as the military assumed power in the prominent African states of Nigeria and Ghana and later spread to many others, particularly in West Africa and also in East Africa. The corruption of these regimes and the brutality with which they ruled made Africa a sorry spectacle. In those African states where, for a variety of reasons, the military never assumed power—such as Kenya, Malawi, and Zambia—state hegemony, usually under the auspices of single-party arrangements, stifled political life. These one-party systems often degenerated into what Robert H. Jackson and Carl C. Rosberg aptly described as personal rule.[6]

These conditions worsened during the first two decades of African political independence, and they created an environment in which, as Hermet was earlier quoted as saying, churches were the only organizations that had not only survived the predatory practices of the state but also had enough resources to directly engage it. Church-state conflict erupted in the late 1980s, fueled in part by the collapse of the Soviet Union and the Eastern European one-party political systems and the role churches played in that process.[7] The churches generally called for an end to the monopolization of power by a few and for the introduction of political pluralism. The assumption was that political pluralism would rejuvenate sterile political systems and increase their ability to deliver public goods. There was also an apparent hope that pluralist politics would reduce the incidence of violent coups and rebellions and infuse sanity into the politics of Africa.

Although Benin was probably the first African country to be led to political pluralism by a clerical figure,[8] Zambia, as shown in chapter 2, is often cited as the first major country to experience a peaceful transition from single-party rule to multiparty politics. The nonviolent election that ended Kenneth Kaunda's twenty-seven-year rule was said to be a "noteworthy achievement."[9] It appeared to mark the beginning of a new era of peaceful politics in Africa. "For once government had changed hands without (revolutionary or military) violence and without military force (or its threat) being required to underwrite the results of the election."[10] The role churches played in this process did not go unnoticed. Jimmy Carter, who was in Zambia as an observer during this time, describes how churches helped defuse a constitutional conflict that almost derailed the process:

[The] elections were threatened by a political impasse: Frederick Chiluba's Movement for Multiparty Democracy was determined to boycott the elections unless important sections of the constitution were redrafted and adopted . . . Zambian president Kenneth Kaunda of the United National Independence Party and Mr. Chiluba agreed to meet in the Anglican Cathedral in Lusaka. The church provided an acceptable meeting place for both parties. Their meeting, which began with shared prayer, resulted eventually in a redrafting of the constitution that opened the way for the elections. Later, during the actual elections, members of churches provided invaluable cooperation in the training and deployment of Zambian election monitors for virtually every polling site. The churches carried the trust of the Zambian people and made a decisive contribution to the reestablishment of democracy.[11]

Churches have also played a major role in other African countries. The experience of Malawi was in many ways similar to that of Zambia. Kamuzu Banda came to office in 1964 and held on to power for three decades. His political opponents were either killed or forced into exile. By the 1990s, all political opposition movements had been liquidated; no one dared challenge Banda's Malawi Congress Party. In 1992, the Catholic bishops of Malawi issued statements in which they criticized Banda's government for failing to deliver efficient social services and, more importantly, highlighted the lack of democratic expression in the country. Banda's regime was alarmed. The statements were declared seditious, the bishops placed under house arrest, and their lives threatened. However, Banda's reaction triggered international criticism and stirred latent internal opposition. Banda was voted out of office in 1994: thus, "the Catholic bishops were accidental prophets and midwives of the birth of democracy in Malawi."[12]

Zaire, now the Republic of Congo, has been described as an "African horror" story.[13] Crawford Young and Thomas Turner, who have examined the political development of this country since Mobutu Sese Seko assumed power through a military coup in 1965, identified five stages in the reign of Mobutu: (1) power seizure, (2) consolidation, (3) ascendancy, (4) state expansion, and (5) crisis and decay.[14] Although there were earlier philosophical conflicts between Mobutu's regime and the Catholic Church, it was in the "crisis and decay" stage that church-state rivalry became actuated.[15] In 1990 a church-initiated national conference was called to try to bring about democratization in the country. When the government abruptly suspended the proceedings of this conference, churches in the country's capital, Kinshasa, organized a "Peace and Hope" rally at which many carried Bibles and rosaries. However, government troops opened fire, killing at least thirty people and wounding over one hundred. Mobutu's information minister, Kitenge Yezu, blamed "radical Roman Catholic priests," who, he said, "were totally responsible for what happened as they had been warned not to hold the march."[16] Although Mobutu was ultimately ousted by an armed rebellion led by Laurent Kabila, churches had previously taken courageous steps in an effort to bring about peaceful change.

Kenya was for a long time presented as the most successful African country in both political and economic terms. However, as the ruling Kenya African National Union (KANU) eliminated all political opposition, it eventually found itself in direct confrontation with churches. David Troup, who has traced the increasing political activism of churches in Kenya since Daniel arap Moi came to power in 1978, observed that "churches . . . occupied the ground emptied by the silencing of serious political opposition."[17] G. P. Benson has also explored the ideological conflicts between the churches and the political leadership of Kenya.[18] The most dramatic church-state clashes started in the mid 1980s, when the National Council of Churches of Kenya (NCCK) openly criticized the state over its maneuvers to reduce privacy in voting and to limit the autonomy of the judiciary. The NCCK's publication, *Beyond*, ridiculed the KANU-engineered election of 1988. The publication was banned and the editor jailed. In 1990 the NCCK published a paper called "A Kairos for Kenya" in which it called for change. By 1991, a pro-democracy movement had emerged in Kenya which pressured the government to adopt multiparty politics. That the churches favored political pluralism is made clear by the political education materials that they produced at this time, which included such topics as "Towards Multiparty Democracy in Kenya" and "Multi-Party Electoral Process in Kenya."[19] Kenya adopted a pluralist constitution in 1992.

The churches also played a similar role in Namibia—the southwest African coastal territory which was once a Germany colony but was later occupied by South Africa in defiance of the United Nations. Peter H. Katjavivi has detailed the evolution of church involvement in the Namibian politics of independence.[20] In a more recent study, Philip Steenkamp has observed that the churches were "drawn into the growing political vacuum created by the repression of black opposition . . . and found [themselves] at the forefront of internal resistance to the state."[21] This is because many church leaders identified with the desire for self-determination. Writing in the late 1980s, Barney Pityana provided a vivid description of the role of the churches in Namibia's politics of independence: "The pastors often interceded for the people, marched with them, endured suffering just as they did. Not a few pastors and Christians . . . have been martyred. Church property has been razed to the ground by arsonists. Pastors have been refused passports. The suffering of the people has likewise been the experience of the church."[22]

Thus, by the time of independence in 1990, the Christian Council of Namibia had become the de facto internal arm of the South West African People's Organization (SWAPO), the formerly exiled liberation movement that assumed power at independence.[23] Namibia is, therefore, another country in Africa in which churches played a critical role in bringing about political change.

THE UNCERTAIN ROLE OF CHURCHES IN PLURALIST AFRICA

The ending of apartheid in South Africa and the adoption of political pluralism in many African states has created a sense of optimism in Africa and internationally. Speaking in support of his Africa trade initiative, United States President, Bill Clinton, catalogued these promising developments:

Since 1990, the number of democracies in sub-Saharan Africa has more than quadrupled. Now more than half of the region's states have freely chosen their leaders. Many are embracing economic reform, opening markets, privatizing, stabilizing their currencies. Growth has more than tripled since 1990. The economies in such countries as Senegal, Ethiopia, Ghana, Mozambique, Cote d'Ivoire are expanding at rates up to seven percent. Ethiopia was not long ago gripped by famine; it grew 12 percent last year. Uganda, once a byword for tragedy, has become a magnet for investment; it grew almost 10 percent last year.[24]

Africa, therefore, enters the new century with renewed hope. Some people, such as South Africa's president, Thabo Mbeki, now talk of an African "renaissance"—an era in which Africa's political and economic life will be transformed. However, despite calls for a Christian contribution to this renaissance, the role of the churches in pluralist Africa is uncertain.[25] The ending of state repression and the activation of civil society appears to have made political involvement by churches redundant. In South Africa, for instance, some have wondered whether the churches will be "confined to being ignored and a peripheral force." [26] This fear is strengthened by the departure of many church leaders from the SACC. Frank Chikane, for example, left his leadership position in the SACC in 1994, claiming the victory over apartheid was a "mission accomplished."[27] The result is that SACC is "no longer as publicly prominent as it was during the struggle."[28]

In Zambia, where, as noted above, the churches were actively involved in the ending of one-party rule and the introduction of political pluralism, there are strong indicators that the role of the churches is no longer certain. The Evangelical Fellowship of Zambia, which was deeply involved in the transition of 1991,[29] issued a statement asking its member churches to disengage from politics.[30] Thus, while the churches were united in monitoring the election of 1991, they have shown little interest in the electoral process since then. If anything, church leaders who were united over the ending of state repression are now divided on partisan grounds.[31] One Zambian church leader has written that the church in Zambia is "grappling" for "a sense of direction" and needs to "reassert its role in the nation."[32]

It is the loss of direction and purpose that this chapter seeks to address. The argument is that the demise of one-party rule and military dictatorship and the demolition of apartheid in South Africa does not mark the end of the role of churches in Africa's political life. This chapter supports Gruchy's conviction that "just as the . . . churches played an important role in the struggle for liberation and in some instances functioned as the midwife of democratic transition, so [they are] now called to participate in the renewal of Africa."[33] The proposition is critical because political pluralism actually poses a new challenge for the ecclesiastical bodies as it creates an environment in which political conflict can more easily occur. It must be remembered that the one-party state and military dictatorship emerged in part as a response to the real or potential threat to peace that competitive politics posed. The turmoil that has been seen in Kenya since pluralism was reintroduced and the chaos that has occasionally rocked Zambia since 1991 are indicators of the fragility that democratization has introduced into African political systems.

HOW PLURALISM THREATENS PEACE IN AFRICA

Churches have supported democratization because, among other things, they believe that competitive politics will reduce political tensions within African nations and possibly eliminate the all too common resort to arms to bring about political change. The appeal of this way of thinking is not hard to see. Most conflicts in Africa have been connected to the lack of alternative means of bringing about change. Political opposition movements have had to resort to civil war to end the regimes of Mobutu in Zaire, Idi Amin in Uganda, Samuel Doe in Liberia, Haile Mariam Mengistu in Ethiopia, and many others. In other cases, such as Angola and Mozambique, ethnic and ideological differences have led to long-lasting civil wars that have cost millions of lives. It is against this backdrop that transitions to pluralist politics have been welcomed as processes that foster peace and eliminate conflict. As Anthony Lake, National Security Advisor to President Clinton, put it: "African leaders must make room—indeed, invite—a flourishing local opposition. It is in their interest to allow this opposition to grow . . . because it provides a safety valve for discontent, a way to express another opinion that does not involve an AK-47, a mortar or a mine."[34] This optimism about democracy and global peace has also been expressed by Ronald J. Glossop.[35]

Nonetheless, a closer scrutiny reveals that while pluralism is certainly desirable, it is not the ultimate panacea for conflict in Africa. First, pluralism could trigger forms of conflict that single-party systems and military rule may have helped contain. For example, tribal and ethnic cleavages that may have been contained by centralized political control could resurface. In Kenya, for example, pluralism has been accompanied by ethnic and regional conflicts. Such incidents were relatively absent during single-party rule. In Nigeria, attempts to introduce political pluralism have been marred by regional, ethnic, and religious tensions resulting in military intervention.[36]

Second, peace in pluralist Africa is also threatened by the tendency of

those elected into power to seek vengeance against those who were previously in power. Opponents of Frederick Chiluba of Zambia claimed
that the arrest of Kenneth Kaunda was an act of vengeance by Chiluba
who was himself once jailed by Kaunda. "Chiluba . . . is proclaiming
universal Christian love, but persecuting [the opposition] with personal
hatred and vicious vengeance," wrote Akashambatwa Mbikusita Lewa-
nika, a leader of an opposition party in pluralist Zambia.[37] The tendency
to seek retribution against those who were in power before could lead
to new conflict.

Third, since pluralism is designed to reduce the monopolization of
power, it leads to weaker states that may not be able to fend off intrastate
or interstate efforts to topple them. In Sierra Leone, for example, where
the churches "worked so hard"[38] to have a new government elected after
years of power abuse, disgruntled military officers soon overthrew the
new government, plunging the country into further turmoil. The elected
government was eventually restored, but only after much fighting. The
reduction of the power of the state, while increasing societal participation
in governance, also increases the possibility of dissidents creating chaos.
This is particularly so in weak democracies where some factions may
not feel bound by constitutional constraints.

Finally, political pluralism reintroduces the danger of radical and fun-
damentalist religious movements forming political parties and assuming
power. Despite the influence of religion in African social life, most of
Africa has resisted political leadership based purely on religious convictions. Pluralism could reverse this. A.B.K. Kasozi has shown how Christians and Muslims continue to compete for input into policy formulation
in East Africa.[39] In another study, Francois Constanin shows that there
forceful attempts have been made to create Islamic national organizations
in Tanzania, Uganda, and Kenya.[40] In a related article, Donal R. Cruise
O'Brien has examined the phobic reaction of the Kenyan government to
attempts by Muslims to create an Islamic party.[41] Although Kenyan authorities have so far effectively restrained the Muslim population from
forming a party, these studies make it clear that pluralism has made it
possible for such movements to take root in Uganda, Kenya, and Tanzania.

The above examination of how political pluralism may engender further conflict in Africa is illustrative, not exhaustive. It illustrates the
argument made by Robert L. Rothstein that "democracy is hardly a panacea, and it will not by itself either resolve profound domestic problems
. . . or necessarily generate an international order that is more peaceful."[42]

It strengthens the proposition that churches still have a significant role to play in fostering peace in pluralist Africa. This role is more challenging and delicate than that of challenging repressive governments. It is also a role that is unique to Christian churches because it is derived from the core teachings of the faith. And it is a role that has greater potential to bring about peace without compromising the desirable aspects of competitive politics.

PROCLAIMING POLITICS OF LOVE

After years of colonial rule and, more recently, racist domination in Southern Africa, tyrannical authoritarianism in most other countries, and insane civil wars and horrific conflicts almost everywhere, there is no doubt that Africa and its people desire and deserve peace. This chapter has argued that while political pluralism is a hopeful development, it is not the cure-all for the conflict and violence that has often marred the continent's political life. It has been pointed out that pluralistic politics may provoke new sources of conflict. Thus, while the involvement of churches in the transition to multiparty politics is commendable, it still falls short of the potential contribution that the churches can make toward a peaceful and prosperous Africa. The rest of the chapter addresses this question: What role can churches and Christianity play in fostering conflict resolution and promoting peace in pluralist Africa?

In order to address this question effectively, it is imperative that a working definition of what is meant by politics in this context be offered. Such a definition must be sensitive to African culture and accommodate the communal nature of African society. Perhaps the best way to accomplish this is by asking, what is politics about in Africa? Harvey J. Sindima provides an insightful response: "Politics is an everyday reality in which everyone is involved; politics is about how people live together, in a family, village, town or wherever people are. Politics is about how people work together. Politics is about building networks of relations between people; a way people communicate among themselves as they live together."[43]

This understanding of the phenomenon removes the one-sided perception of politics as a soulless struggle for dominance. Instead, this conceptualization of politics brings to the forefront the fact that politics is about community building and peaceful coexistence. Politics is a way for humans to live together and to enrich each other. It is a way of finding means through which humans can commune, and, whenever necessary, resolve communal disagreements without recourse to war. In fact, politics is a continuous process of conflict prevention and resolution for the sake of community building. Africa, and indeed most of the world, is yet to see this kind of political living. In fact, a skeptical reader could say that this conceptualization of politics is too utopian.

However, idealistic commitment to principle can drive people to action. The political power of religion is its ability to transform and propel human behavior through its idealistic invocations and convictions. Much of the political opposition of the African churches to authoritarian rule can rightly be attributed to an idealistic commitment to justice. For instance, during the terrorizing reign of Idi Amin in Uganda, Archbishop Janani Luwum was assassinated for criticizing Amin's despotic rule. In a study of church-state relations in Uganda, Kevin Ward observes that Luwum "died as a witness to the truth for the sake of Christ and as a defender of the rights of the Ugandan people as a whole."[44] The same could be said of the Kenyan bishop, Alexander Muge, who was killed in a mysterious accident following public death threats from state officials for his criticism of the one-party state.[45] The risks taken by such church leaders cannot be explained fully without taking into account their commitment to idealistic religious convictions that certain state-societal relations are simply wrong. Religious conviction is, therefore, a variable in political behavior.

It is this transformative and energizing impact of religion on individual and communal behavior that churches must now bring into Africa's political arena in order to foster peace and defuse the potential conflicts that come with political pluralism. Religion's influence on political behavior is often based on ideas lodged in the sacred teachings of the particular religion. That is why some peace researchers have called for a closer examination of religious texts and traditions as a critical aspect of the development of conflict resolution theories.[46] Ideas that can influence political behavior and foster peaceful democracies are found in biblical writings. Howard John Loewen has shown that all church traditions base their statements on peace on scriptural sources.[47] Therefore, the question for church leaders and followers is this: What do the biblical authors say about politics—or, as Sindima put it, "how people live together."

It is at this point that the Christian concept of love surfaces. Love of other humans is Christianity's response to the question, "How should we live together?" Jesus, Paul N. Anderson writes, "taught the radical notion that the God of love and peace expects God's children also to act in loving and peaceful ways."[48] Paul, the most prolific writer among the early converts to Christianity, also identified love as the best way to build a community. The word *love* as used here refers to a qualitative phenomenon distinct from mere friendship or sexual passion. Glenn Tinder asserts that this love is "based on the nature not of human beings but of God."[49] Since God is selfless, this love (*agape* in the Greek) is also selfless. In his epistle to the Corinthian converts, St. Paul provided the most eloquent description of this love: "Love is patient, love is kind. It does not envy, it does not boast, it is not proud. It is not rude, it is not self-seeking, it is not easily angered, it keeps no record of wrongs. Love does not delight in evil but rejoices with truth. It always protects, always trusts, always hopes, always perseveres."[50]

The relevance of these attributes of selfless love to Africa's pluralist politics is obvious. This love has the power to transform human relationships so that political leaders and movements are less self-seeking—since self-seeking activity often leads to strife and violence—and more committed to building societies characterized by mutual respect. Clearly, such a selfless affection toward other individual and group actors in competitive politics has the power to defuse the conflicts that threaten to ruin the democratic gains that have been made in the last ten years.

That is why, while in the era of authoritarian politics, churches did well to confront the status quo and help bring about the demise of monopolistic rule, in the pluralist environment, churches now have the burden of infusing love as the guiding ethic in the practice of African politics. Furthermore, this is a charge that cannot be compromised because, as Sindima has reiterated, Christians and Christian churches "are the instruments for bringing God's reign in the here and now."[51] The church's power "is from the ONE who established it—God—and the church's duty is to provide people with possibilities for self-transcendence."[52]

HOW CHURCHES CAN FOSTER LOVE

Several factors favor the churches' ability to "provide people with possibilities for self-transcendence" or, in the language of this chapter, to infuse selfless love into the practice of politics. First, Christianity continues to spread rapidly across the continent. As Michael Bratton has observed, churches in Africa are the largest forms of voluntary associations.[53] And Samuel Huntington asserts that "as the numbers of Christians multiply . . . their political power will increase."[54] This pervasiveness of Christianity in Africa means that churches can reach and influence more and more people at the grassroots level. The influence of the love ethic at the grassroots level is critical to peace because it is the people at this level who are often recruited for violent activities when political conflict degenerates into violence. Individuals and communities influenced and motivated by selfless love can resist appeals to join or support groups that use violence to accomplish political goals.

Auspiciously, the influence of the churches is not limited to the grass roots. Adrian Hastings has noted that Christianity in sub-Saharan Africa has historically been "the continent's dominant religion at the level of government and of political life."[55] So churches have the opportunity to communicate the value of selfless love to the elite, whose members have influence in political decision making. Influence at this level is crucial because it is the elite whose members reject election results and mobilizes people at grass roots into violence. It is the elite members who seek vengeance against past and present political rivals. It is they who worsen economic situations by siphoning off a country's resources and creating environments in which disgruntled populations resort to violent means of expression. In other words, churches have both a grave responsibility and also a great opportunity to influence individuals at this level of society with the power of love that is "not self-seeking" and "keeps no record of wrongs."

Church leaders, who once used their pulpits to call for political pluralism, should now use the same platform to proclaim messages of love, peace, reconciliation, and national unity to their congregations. Religious leaders need to make it clear that loving one's neighbors—despite ethnic, regional, and political differences—is a central tenet of the Christian faith. The clergy should integrate this into their perception of their pastoral duties in the communities. Just as it is their work to create harmony in homes and among their congregations, it is also their work to promote harmony on a large scale in the pluralist political situations in which many African nations find themselves in this new century.

The second factor that works in the churches' favor in their effort to infuse love into politics is that churches in Africa have plenty of access to the mass media. Church organizations in almost all African countries either own printing presses or at least have the capacity to publish books, magazines, and newspapers. The Catholic Church, for instance, has strong publishing programs in almost all countries where it has a significant presence. Therefore, as I have argued elsewhere, the churches have a great opportunity to communicate the love ethic through the print media.[56] Church publishing houses should develop editorial programs to deliberately include books, magazines, and pamphlets that address love as an integral element of Christian witness. Such publications should call readers to love their neighbors and educate them about peace and reconciliation. Mambo Press in Zimbabwe was aggressive in publishing books that promoted reconciliation and coexistence during the liberation war in what was then Southern Rhodesia. The conflicts over land ownership that erupted again in Zimbabwe in early 2000 indicate that Mambo Press's challenge is far from over.

The churches also either own community radio stations or at least have access to radio. The broadcast media can also be employed to communicate the value of love in politics and help contain the public response to disgruntled political leaders who may want to resort to violence. Samie Ikechi Ihejirika has pointed out that peace researchers and workers in Africa must "pay special attention to the media . . . because of their potential to create fear, distrust and panic among the people."[57] Ihejirika's fears are confirmed by the Rwandan experience where the violence was, at least partly, fueled by the mass media. In President Clinton's words, "The ground for violence was carefully prepared, the airwaves poisoned with hate, casting the Tutsis as scapegoats for problems of Rwanda, denying their humanity. All of this was done clearly, to make it easy for otherwise reluctant people to participate."[58] If the airwaves can be "poisoned with hate" and used to draw reluctant participants into violent activity, that they also can be purified with love and used to affirm the stance of those not willing to hurt their neighbors. Christian radio broadcasts that are transmitted across the nations, such as those of Transworld Radio, could beam messages of love and peace to countries where political strife is brewing.

Television is another avenue through which the churches can touch African society with the Christian message of love. Although people living in rural Africa may not have access to television, a significant number of urban Africans receive at least a few hours of television broadcasting daily. Because of the standing of the churches in African society, church leaders often appear on national television stations and are asked to address issues of significance to society. Such appearances can be opportunities for religious figures to promote love. In other words, churches can and should use the media to contribute to peace in pluralist Africa.

Another practical way for churches to infuse love into society may be through public rhetoric—rhetoric understood here as "the persuasive presentation of argument"[59]—to persuade members and leaders of political movements of the superiority of the politics of love over the politics of hate that often leads to violence. Such rhetoric will serve a dual purpose. First, it will be *prescriptive* in the sense that church spokespersons will be declaring love of other people, including political opponents, as the means to Africa's present and future political well-being. This prescription is not designed to decrease competitiveness in politics, as this is a desirable element of good governance, but to decrease the number of purely egocentric demands which lead only to chaos and further conflict. Second, such rhetoric will serve a *demonstrative* function. By using rhetorical efforts, church spokespersons will affirm the approach to politics that employs persuasive arguments to influence the polity, rather than, say, intimidation, bribery, and other activities that African political leaders often resort to, to gain or retain a following. Church spokespersons can display the power of rhetoric by arguing at public meetings or conferences and in the media that loving other people selflessly is the key to creating a desirable political life. If, as will most likely be the case, more and more people are persuaded that love and peace are preferable in politics, it may also dawn upon political leaders that they too can use rhetoric to accomplish their political goals. And, if more political leaders adopt rhetoric as a tool for accomplishing political goals, the chances of resorting to undesirable means are greatly reduced. One good example here is Bishop Desmond Tutu of South Africa who has used rhetoric unwaveringly to promote reconciliation in the new South Africa.

Churches must also be more aggressive in providing peace education in schools, colleges, universities, and seminaries. The churches should emulate the Carter Center's efforts to promote peace education in Ethiopian and Liberian schools.[60] Churches in Africa operate a plethora of schools, colleges, universities, seminaries, and other training institutions. Programs in church-sponsored institutions should include peace education. One good example of such an effort is the one-year course in peace building offered by the pan-African center in Kitwe, Zambia, called the Mindolo Ecumenical Foundation. The program, which attracts participants from across Africa, was developed "in response to the many destructive conflicts that are facing the Africa continent."[61] Clearly, the continent needs more such programs and there is no better source of peace education than the churches, whose primary driving force is love.

Another way for churches to infuse love into African societies is for them to play a visible role in peace and reconciliation conferences and efforts. Bishop Tutu's role in the Truth and Reconciliation Commission in South Africa deserves mention. Tutu's neutrality and his fervent commitment to love of all South Africans—Black, White, Coloured, or Asian—helped sustain the reconciliation process even when it faced much criticism.[62] In Liberia, churches hosted a number of national reconciliation events at the height of the grisly conflict in that country. Although those conferences never got much international publicity and did not lead to a truce between the warring parties, they did infuse a sense of hope in the millions of Liberians beleaguered in the war-torn nation. The church leaders who put these efforts together pointed to love and reconciliation as the ultimate response to Liberia's conflict.

Providing relief and development aid in a respectful and loving way and without bias is another way churches can demonstrate love in societies whose struggles with poverty are aggravated by civil strife and political rivalry. It is not uncommon in pluralist Africa for a region of a country to be denied relief and development aid because the majority of the people living there are perceived as political opponents of those in power. In the Sudan, for example, non-Muslims claim state relief agencies do not deliver aid to non-Muslim regions of the country, particularly the South, which has been fighting for secession since 1955. But even in relatively stable and pluralist African states such as Zambia, Kenya, and Senegal, constituencies that are represented by opposition members are often denied state-administered relief and development aid. It is in this context that churches can exhibit true Christian love by offering relief services and development programs to people regardless of religious, ethnic, and political affiliation. In this way, churches can show that Christian love is not just an abstract concept but that it leads to tangible benefits for societies in which it is practiced.

Finally, churches have the opportunity to bring love into African politics through prayer. A social scientist who proposes that prayer can help communities develop nonviolent, love-driven political behavior risks ridicule. This aversion toward prayer is quite understandable. Prayer is a concept that is grossly misused by those who purport to practice it and, therefore, generally ignored by those seeking to promote peaceful politics. Nonetheless, the renewed interest in religion as the "missing dimension" of conflict analysis and resolution and the calls in the literature for further research into the role of religious movements in peacemaking necessitates a closer scrutiny of the practice of prayer.[63] Since this chapter is focused on Christian churches, the idea of prayer and its potential impact on political behavior will be examined from a Christian perspective.

Sindima provides an understanding of prayer that is most relevant to the propositions of this chapter. He accomplishes this by painting two portraits of prayer. The first is the type of prayer he calls "empty talk," which has no social impact. This kind of prayer has no relevance to peacemaking: "A prayer that does not initiate one into some kind of action, a transformation, a conversion, is empty talk. At best such prayer is therapy, an emotional catharsis that makes one feel good because deep inner feelings have been verbalized. That cannot be talking to and listening to God, but a need to hear oneself."[64]

Although this kind of prayer may have therapeutic benefits, it has little relevance to creating communities whose politics are governed by love. The other kind of prayer, however, has monumental implications for both individual practitioners and the community. It is transformative and has a boundless potential for influencing politics. Here is how it is described. "Prayer is a silent revolution against evil in all its manifestations, individual and structural. To pray is to say the world is not as God intended it to be; it is no longer as good as it was at creation. To pray is to acknowledge that people have corrupted the world and that the whole creation groans as it awaits liberation. Prayer is ushering the rule of God into one's life and the world."[65]

This understanding of prayer makes it easier to advance the argument that churches can contribute to peaceful politics in pluralist Africa through public and private prayer for love in politics. Prayer is, in a sense, a private and public declaration of a preference for and a commitment to a cause. For example, in South Africa, church leaders revealed their opposition to the apartheid regime by praying against it, causing a stir in political circles.[66] This is because prayer is, in a sense, a powerful statement to oneself, to God, and to the community reiterating one's position in a conflictual situation. Prayer for love and peace in politics effectively complements the churches' rhetorical input recommended earlier. Private and public prayer for love and peace strengthens the credibility of the churches' rhetoric on love and infuses it with a sincere passion. Therefore, the invitation to prayer is not a "form of flight from the world, but getting involved in the world by being God's agent for change."[67]

CONCLUSION

This chapter has a simple objective: to identify a unique role for churches to play in Africa in the pluralist era. It acknowledges the significance played by churches in the transitions to political pluralism that have swept across the continent in the 1990s. Through a brief examination of some cases, it shows how, in most cases, churches often emerged as the only viable civil society movement with the capacity to challenge authoritarian states. The vacuum created by the liquidation of opposition movements appears to be the principal factor that triggered the political activism of ecclesiastical bodies in most countries. Once the transition to plural politics was achieved, the churches lost their distinctive political role and were threatened with either political irrelevance or fragmentation into the partisan divisions that now characterize pluralistic Africa.

The coming of plural politics in Africa has created a sense of optimism for the continent. The assumption is that pluralism will defuse the political conflicts that have so often in the past plunged the continent into upheavals. In other words, pluralism is presumed to bring peace to Africa's political life. Yet, pluralism, especially operating in an environment where there are no strong democratic institutions, traditions, and facilities, could foster further conflict. Therefore, the contention of this chapter is that churches should come back to the political arena and infuse Africa's plural politics with love. Love, or a selfless commitment to public service, is apparently absent from African politics. Love has the power to introduce sanity into Africa's pluralist experiment and lead the continent to further political and economic prosperity in the new century.

NOTES

1. Quoted in Mattei Dogan and Domnique Pelassy, *How to Compare Nations: Strategies in Comparative Politics* (Chatham, NJ: Chatham House Publishers, 1984), 35.

2. Stefan Lovgren, "It Takes a Dictatorship to Raise a Democracy," *US News and World Report* (23 March 1998), 41.

3. M. Darrol Bryant, "Planetary Society: Meditations on Peace in a Planetary Society," *International Journal on World Peace* 13, 1 (March 1996): 40.

4. Richard L. Johnson and Eric Ledbetter, " 'Spiritualizing the Political': Christ and Christianity in Gandhi's Satyagraha," *Peace and Change* 22, 1 (January 1997): 32–47.

5. Ibid., 44.

6. Robert H. Jackson and Carl G. Rosberg, "Personal Rule: Theory and Practice in Africa," *Comparative Politics* 16 (July 1984): 421–442.

7. See David Steel, "At the Front Lines of the Revolution: East Germany's Churches Give Sanctuary and Succor to the Purveyors of Change," in Douglas

Johnstone and Cynthia Samson, *Religion, The Missing Dimension of Statecraft* (New York: Oxford University Press, 1994), 88–118.

8. For a report, see Margaret Novicki, "Msgr. Isidore de Souza: Building a New Benin," *Africa Report* (May 1991), 43–45.

9. Keith Panter-Brick, "Prospects for Democracy in Zambia," *Government and Opposition* 29, 2 (Spring 1994): 231.

10. Carolyn Baylies and Morris Szeftel, "The Fall and Rise of Multiparty Politics in Zambia," *Review of African Political Economy*, no. 54 (July 1992): 75.

11. Jimmy Carter, "Foreword," in Johnstone and Samson, eds., *Religion, The Missing Dimension of Statecraft.*

12. Silas Ncozana, "The Church's Engagement with Political and Social Issues: The Perspective of the Church in Malawi," *Church and Society* (March–April 1995): 36.

13. Bill Berkeley, "Zaire: An African Horror Story," *The Atlantic* (August 1993).

14. Crawford Young and Thomas Turner, *The Rise and Decline of the Zairian State* (Madison: University of Wisconsin Press, 1985), 47.

15. Ngindu Mushete, "Authenticity and Christianity in Zaire," in *Christianity in Independent Africa*, ed. Edward Fashole-Luke et al. (Bloomington: Indiana University Press, 1978), 228–241.

16. *Lutheran World Information* (September 1992).

17. David Throup, "Render unto Caesar the Things That Are Caesar's: The Politics of Church-State Conflict in Kenya 1978–1990," in *Religion and Politics in East Africa*, ed. Holger Bernt Hansen and Michael Twaddle. (Athens, OH: Ohio University Press, 1995), 143–176.

18. G. P. Benson, "Ideological Politics versus Biblical Hermeneutics: Kenya's Protestant Churches and the Nyayo State," in *Religion and Politics in East Africa*, ed. Hansen and Twaddle, 143–176.

19. Samuel Kobia, "Promoting Democracy in Africa: Experiences and Future Perspectives," *Church and Society* (March–April 1995): 24–29.

20. Peter H. Katjavivi, "The Role of the Church in the Struggle for Independence," in *Church and Liberation in Namibia*, ed. Peter Katjavivi et al. (London: Pluto Press, 1989), 3–26.

21. Philip Steenkamp, "The Churches," in *Namibia's Liberation Struggle: The Two-Edged Sword*, ed. Colin Leys and John S. Saul, (Athens: Ohio University Press, 1995), 95.

22. Barney Pityana, "Foreword," in Peter Katjavivi et al.

23. Steenkamp, 94.

24. William Clinton, "Remarks Announcing the Africa Trade Initiative," *Weekly Compilation of Presidential Documents* 30, 40 (23 June 1997): 898.

25. John de Gruchy, "Christian Witness at a Time of African Renaissance," *Ecumenical Review* 49, 4 (October 1997): 476–482.

26. John M. Lamola, "Change Is Pain: A Projective Reflection of the Mission

of the Church in South Africa beyond 1994," *International Review of Mission* (January 1994).

27. "Chikane to Leave Council of Churches," *Christian Century* (27 July–3 August 1994), 717.

28. John De Gruchy, "Church Unity and Democratic Transformation: Perspective on Ecclesiology and Ethics in South Africa," *Ecumenical Review* 49, 3 (July 1997): 361.

29. Isaac Phiri, "Evangelical Wins Peaceful Election," *Christianity Today* (16 December 1991), 70.

30. Joseph Imakando, "Resolutions of the 20th–21st March 1992 Political Seminar on the Role of the Church in Politics" (Lusaka: Evangelical Fellowship of Zambia, 1992).

31. Isaac Phiri, "President Disappoints Christians," *Christianity Today* (2 March 1998), 76–77.

32. Bwalya Melu, "Expectation Dwarfed by Realities," *Vision Forum* (November/December 1995).

33. De Gruchy, "Christian Witness at a Time of African Renaissance," *Ecumenical Review* 49, 4 (October 1997): 476–482.

34. Anthony Lake, "U.S. Support for Democracy in Africa," *U.S. Department of State Dispatch* (9 January 1995), 18.

35. Ronald J. Glossop, "Democratic Politics: Alternative to War within Nation-States and Planet Earth," *Peace Research* 29, 3 (August 1997): 26–30.

36. For analyses of the Nigerian transitions to pluralism, see Chudi P. Uwazurike, "Confronting Potential Breakdown: The Nigerian Redemocratization Process," *Journal of Modern African Studies* 28, 1 (March 1990): 55–77, and Pita Ogaba Agbese, "The Impending Demise of Nigeria's Forthcoming Third Republic," *Africa Today* 37, 3 (Third Quarter, 1990), 23–44.

37. *The Post* (Lusaka, Zambia), (30 December 1997).

38. Personal correspondence from Rev. Arnold Temple.

39. A.B.K. Kasozi, "Christian-Muslim Inputs into Public Policy Formulation in Kenya, Tanzania and Uganda," in *Religion and Politics in East Africa* ed. Hansen and Twaddle, 223–246.

40. Francois Constantin, "Muslims and Politics: The Attempts to Create Muslim National Organizations in Tanzania, Uganda and Kenya," in *Religion and Politics in East Africa*, ed. Hansen and Twaddle, 19–31.

41. Donal B. Cruise O'Brien, "Coping with the Christians: The Muslim Predicament in Kenya," in *Religion and Politics in East Africa*, ed. Hansen and Twaddle, 200–219.

42. Robert L. Rothstein, "Week Democracy and the Prospect for Peace and Prosperity in the Third World," *Resolving Third World Conflict: Challenges for a New Era*, ed. in Sheryl J. Brown and Kimber M. Schraub (Washington, DC: United States Peace Institute Press, 1992), 17.

43. Harvey J. Sindima, *Religious and Political Ethics in Africa: A Moral Inquiry* (Westport, CT: Greenwood Press, 1998), 16.

44. Kevin Ward, "The Church of Uganda amidst Conflict: The Interplay between Church and Politics in Uganda since 1962," in *Religion and Politics in East Africa*, ed. Hansen and Twaddle (Athens: Ohio University Press, 1995), 85.

45. Throup, 168–171.

46. See Marc Gopin, "Religion, Violence, and Conflict Resolution," *Peace and Change: A Journal of Peace Research* 22, 1 (January 1997): 1–31.

47. Howard John Loewen, "An Analysis of the Use of Scripture in the Churches' Documents on Peace," *The Church's Peace Witness* ed. in Marlin E. Miller and Barbara Nelson Gingerich (Grand Rapids, MI: Eerdmans, 1994), 15–69.

48. Paul N. Anderson, "Jesus and Peace," in Miller and Gingerich, 110.

49. Glenn Tinder, *The Political Meaning of Christianity* (New York: HarperCollins, 1991), 20.

50. I Corinthians 13: 4–5.

51. Sindima, 185.

52. Ibid., 117.

53. Michael Bratton, "Beyond the State: Civil Society and Associational Life in Africa," *World Politics* 41, 3 (April 1989), 426.

54. Samuel P. Huntington, *The Third Wave: Democratization in the Late Twentieth Century* (Norman: University of Oklahoma Press, 1991), 281.

55. Adrian Hastings, *A History of African Christianity 1950–1975* (New York: Cambridge University Press, 1979), 18.

56. Isaac Phiri, "Publish for Africa's Hope and Future," *Interlit: The International Magazine of Christian Publishing* (April 1998): 6–7.

57. Samie Ikechi Ihejirika, "The Challenges for Peace Education in Post-Cold War Africa," *Peace Research* 29, 1 (February 1997): 107.

58. *New York Times* (26 March 1998), A10.

59. William Safire, *Safire's Political Dictionary* (New York: Ballantine Books, 1978), 611.

60. See Isaac Phiri, *Carter and Africa: Pre-presidential to Post-presidential Years* (Atlanta: Mercer University Press, forthcoming).

61. Personal correspondence with Janet P. Schmidt, coordinator of Peace Education at Mindolo Ecumenical Foundation.

62. For a complete report, see *Truth and Reconciliation Commission of South Africa Report* (New York: Grove, 1999).

63. See Edward Luttwak, "The Missing Dimension," in *Religion: The Missing Dimension of Statecraft*, ed. Johnstone and Samson, 8–19.

64. Sindima, 180.

65. Ibid.

66. See Allan A. Boesak and Charles Villa-Vicencio, eds., *When Prayer Makes News*, (Philadelphia: Westminister Press, 1986).

67. Sindima, 181.

Selected Bibliography

Abraham, Garth. *The Catholic Church and Apartheid: The Response of the Catholic Church in South Africa to the First Decade of National Party Rule 1948–1957.* Johannesburg: Ravan Press, 1989.

Adelman, Kenneth Lee. "The Church-State Conflict in Zaire: 1969–1974." *African Studies Review* 18 (1) (April 1975): 102–116.

Afigbo, A. E. "The Missions, the State and Education in South-Eastern Nigeria, 1950–1967." In *Christianity in Independent Africa*, ed. Edward Fashole-Luke et al. Bloomington: Indiana University Press, 1978.

Ahanotu, Austin. "Muslims and Christians in Nigeria: A Contemporary Political Discourse." In *Religion, State and Society in Contemporary Africa: Nigeria, Sudan, South Africa, Zaire and Mozambique*, ed. Austin Ahanotu. New York: Peter Lang, 1992.

Ainsworth James. "Smile, the Beloved Country: Your Time Has Come," *Africa Today* 41 (1) (1994): 65–68.

Alberts, Louw, and Frank Chikane, eds. *The Road to Rustenberg: The Church Looking forward to a New South Africa.* Cape Town: Struik, 1991.

Alpers, Edward A. "The Struggle for Socialism in Mozambique: 1960–1972." In *Socialism in Sub-Saharan Africa: A New Assessment*, ed. Carl G. Rosberg and Thomas M. Callaghy. Berkeley, CA: Institute of International Studies, 1979.

Anglian, Douglas G., and Timothy M. Shaw. *Zambia's Foreign Policy: Studies in Diplomacy and Dependence.* Boulder, CO: Westview Press, 1979.

Atieno-Odhiambo, E. S. "Origins of the Zimbabwe Problem, 1888–1923." In *Zimbabwe Now*. Rex Collins: London, 1972.

Balia, Daryl. "The Witness of the Methodist Church in South Africa." *International Review of Mission* (01 January 1994): 163–165.

Bantugwa, Ives. "The Role of the Church in the Democratization Process in

Africa: The Zambian Experience." *The Courier* 134 (July–August 1992): 69–71.

Barrel, Howard. " 'The Turn to the Masses': The African National Congress Strategic Review of 1978–79." *Journal of Southern African Studies* 18 (1) (01 March, 1992): 64–92.

Batista, Israel. "Civil Society: A Paradigm or a New Slogan." *The Ecumenical Review* 46 (1) (January 1994): 12–20.

Bayart, Jean-François. "La Fonction Politique des Eglises au Cameroon." *Revue Francaise de Science Politique* 3, (3 June 1973): 514–536.

Beetham, T. A. *Christianity and the New Africa.* New York: Praeger, 1967.

Benson, G. P. "Ideological Politics versus Biblical Hermeneutics: Kenya's Protestant Churches and the Nyayo State." In *Religion and Politics in East Africa*, ed. Holger Bernt Hansen and Michael Twaddle. Athens: Ohio University Press, 1995.

Berkeley, Bill. "Zaire: An African Horror Story." *The Atlantic* (August 1993).

Bhebhe, Ngwabi. "The Evangelical Lutheran Church in Zimbabwe and the War of Liberation, 1975–1980." In *Church and State in Zimbabwe*, ed. Carl F. Hallencreutz and Ambrose M. Moyo. Harare: Mambo Press, 1988.

Boesak, Allan A., and Charles Villa-Vicencio, eds. *When Prayer Makes News.* Philadelphia: Westminster Press, 1986.

Bond, George, et al., eds. *African Christianity: Patterns of Religious Continuity.* New York: Academic Press, 1979.

Borer. "Challenging the State: Churches as Political Actors in South Africa." *Journal of Church and State* 35 (2) (Spring 1993): 229–325.

Bourdillon, M.F.C., ed. *Christianity South of the Zambezi.* Vol. 2. Harare: Mambo Press, 1977.

Bourdillon, Michael, and Paul Gumdani. "Rural Christians and the Zimbabwe Liberation War: A Case Study." In *Church and State in Zimbabwe*, ed. Carl F. Hallencreutz and Ambrose M. Moyo. Harare: Mambo Press, 1988.

Bratton, Michael. "Beyond the State: Civil Society and Associational Life in Africa." *World Politics* 41, (3) (April 1989): 407–430.

———. "Non-Governmental Organizations in Africa: Can They Influence Public Policy?" In *The Changing Politics of Non-Governmental Organizations in African States*, ed. Eve Sanberg. Westport, CT: Praeger, 1994.

Breaking the Chains. West Midlands, U.K.: Christian Vision, 1992. Video.

Brown, Robert McAfee. *Kairos: Three Prophetic Challenges to the Church.* Grand Rapids, MI: Eerdmans, 1990.

Brown, Sheryl J. and Kimber M. Schraub, eds. *Resolving Third World Conflict: Challenges for a New Era.* Washington, DC: United States Peace Institute Press, 1992.

Brown, William Eric. *The Catholic Church in South Africa: From Its Origins to the Present Day.* London: Burns and Oates, 1960.

Bryant, M. Darrol. "Planetary Society: Meditations on Peace in a Planetary Society." *International Journal on World Peace* 13 (1) (March 1996).

Burdette, Marcia M. *Zambia: Between Two Worlds*. Boulder, CO: Westview Press, 1988.

Burnell, Peter. "Zambia at the Crossroads." *World Affairs* 157 (1) (Summer 1994): 19–29.

Catholic Commission for Justice and Peace in Zimbabwe. *The Man in the Middle: Torture, Resettlement and Eviction*. Harare: Catholic Commission for Justice and Peace, 1975.

Chabal, Patrick. *Power in Africa: An Essay in Political Interpretation*. New York: St. Martin's Press, 1994.

Charton, Nancy. "The Witness of the Church of the Province of Southern Africa." *International Review of Mission*. (January 1994): 153–157.

Chikane, Frank, and Louw Alberts. *The Road to Rustenberg: The Church Looking forward to a New South Africa*. Cape Town: Struik, 1991.

Chisala, Beatwell S. *Coup Attempt*. Lusaka: Printed by the Author, 1991.

Concerned Evangelicals. *Evangelical Witness in South Africa*. Grand Rapids, MI: Eerdmans, 1986.

Constantin, Francois. "Muslims and Politics: The Attempts to Create Muslim National Organizations in Tanzania." In *Religion and Politics in East Africa*, ed. Holger Bernt Hansen et al. Athens: Ohio University Press, 1995.

Cook, David J. "The Influence of the Livingstonia Mission upon the Formation of Welfare Associations in Zambia, 1912–31." In *Themes in the Christian History of Central Africa*, ed. Terence Ranger and John Weller. Los Angeles: University of California Press, 1975.

Cooke, Colman M. "Church, State and Education: The Eastern Nigeria Experience, 1950–1967." In *Christianity in Independent Africa*, ed. Edward Fashole-Luke et al. Bloomington: University of Indiana Press, 1978.

Costea, Peter. "Church-State Relations in the Marxist-Leninist Regimes of the Third World. *Journal of Church and State* 32 (2) (Spring 1990): 281–308.

Cross, Sholto. "Independent Churches and Independent States: Jehovah's Witnesses in East and Central Africa." In *Christianity in Independent Africa*, ed. Edward Fashole-Luke, et al. Bloomington: University of Indiana Press, 1978.

Dachs, Anthony J., ed. *Christianity South of the Zambezi*. Vol. 1. Harare: Mambo Press, 1973.

David, Jeffrey. *The Peace in Southern Africa. The Lancaster House Conference on Rhodesia, 1979*. Boulder, CO: Westview Press, 1984.

Davis, R. Hunt, ed. *Apartheid Unravels*. Gainesville: University of Florida Press, 1991.

De Gruchy, John. *The Church Struggle in South Africa*. Grand Rapids, MI: Eerdmans, 1979.

——. *Christianity and Democracy: A Theology for a Just World Order*. New York: Cambridge University Press, 1995.

Dogan, Mattei, and Domnique Pelassy. *How to Compare Nations: Strategies in Comparative Politics*. Chatham, NJ: Chatham House Publishers, 1984.

Du Boulay, Shirley. *Tutu: Voice of the Voiceless*. Grand Rapids, MI: Eerdmans, 1988.

Duval, Raymond D., and John F. Freeman. "The State and Dependent Capitalism." *International Studies Quarterly* 25 (March 1981): 99–176.

Evangelical Fellowship of South Africa. *A Charter for Mobilizing Evangelical Unity*. Pietermaritzburg: Evangelical Fellowship of South Africa, 1985.

——. *Understanding South Africa: A Study Guide to Help Christians Understand the Social Dynamic from an Evangelical Perspective*. Pietermaritzburg: Evangelical Fellowship of South Africa, 1989.

——. "The EFSA 1990 AGM: Evangelical Unity is Growing." News Release, 26 March 1990. Pietermaritzburg: Evangelical Fellowship of South Africa, 1990.

Fashole-Luke, Edward, et al., eds. *Christianity in Independent Africa*. Bloomington: Indiana University Press, 1978.

Fatton, Robert. *Black Consciousness in South Africa*. New York: State University of New York Press, 1986.

Fredrickson, George M. *Black Liberation: A Comparative History of Black Ideologies in the United States and South Africa*. New York: Oxford University Press, 1995.

Froise, Majorie, ed. *South Central Africa: A Factual Portrait of the Christian Church*. Monrovia, CA; World Vision, 1991.

Frostin, Per. *Liberation Theology in Tanzania and South Africa*. Lund: Lund University Press, 1988.

Gertzel, Cherry, et al., eds. *The Dynamics of the One-Party State in Zambia*. Manchester, NH: Manchester University Press, 1984.

Gifford, Paul. *The Religious Right in Southern Africa*. Harare: Baobab Books, 1988.

——. *Christianity and Politics in Does's Liberia*. New York: Cambridge University Press, 1993.

Gundani, Paul H. "The Catholic Church and National Development in Independent Zimbabwe." In *Church and State in Zimbabwe*, ed. Carl F. Hallencreutz and Ambrose M. Moyo. Harare: Mambo Press, 1988.

Hall, Richard. *Kaunda Founder of Zambia*. London: Longmans, 1964.

Hallencreutz, Carl F. "A Council in Crossfire: ZCC 1964–1980." In *Church and State in Zimbabwe*, ed. Carl F. Hallencreutz and Ambrose M. Moyo. Harare: Mambo Press, 1988.

Hancock, Ian. *The Liberals, Moderates and Radicals in Rhodesia 1953–1980.* New York: St. Martin's Press, 1984.

Hansen, Holger Bernt and Michael Twaddle, eds. *Religion and Politics in East Africa.* Athens: Ohio University Press, 1995.

Hastings, Adrian. "John Lester Membe." In *Themes in the Christian History of Central Africa,* ed. Terence Ranger and John Weller. Los Angeles: University of California Press, 1975.

———. *A History of African Christianity 1950–1975.* New York: Cambridge University Press, 1979.

Hatch, John. *Two African Statesmen: Kaunda of Zambia and Nyerere of Tanzania.* London: Secker and Warburg, 1976.

Herbst, Jeffrey. *State Politics in Zimbabwe.* Los Angeles: University of California Press, 1990.

Hinchcliff, Peter. *The Church in South Africa.* London: SPCK, 1968.

Hope, Marjorie, and James Young. *The South African Churches in a Revolutionary Situation.* New York: Orbis Books, 1981.

Houtart, Francois, and Andre Rousseau. *The Church and Revolution: From the French Revolutions of 1789 to the Paris Riots of 1968; From Cuba to Southern Africa; From Vietnam to Latin America.* New York: Orbis Books, 1971.

Howarth, David. "The Idealogies and Strategies of Resistance in Post-Sharpeville South Africa: Thought on Anthony Marx's Lessons of Struggle." *Africa Today* 41 (1994): 21–38.

Hulley, L. D. "The Churches and Civil Disobedience in South Africa." *Missionalia* (April 1993): 74–85.

Huntington, Samuel P. *The Third Wave: Democratization in the Late Twentieth Century.* Norman: University of Oklahoma Press, 1991.

Iheanyi, Enwerem M. "The Politicization of Religion in Modern Nigeria: The Emergence and Politics of the Christian Association of Nigeria." Ph.D. diss., York University, UK, 1992.

Ilesanmi, Simeon O. "Recent Theories of Religion and Politics in Nigeria." *Journal of Church and State* 37 (2) (Spring 1995): 308–327.

International Commission of Jurists. *Racial Discrimination and Repression in Southern Rhodesia.* London: Catholic Institute for International Relations, 1976.

International Defence and Aid Fund. *Smith's Settlement: Events in Zimbabwe since 3rd March 1978.* London: International Defence and Aid Fund, 1978.

Jackson, Robert H., and Carl G. Rosberg, "Personal Rule: Theory and Practice in Africa." *Comparative Politics* 16 (July 1984): 421–442.

Jenkins, Karen. "The Christian Church as an NGO in Africa: Supporting Post-independence Era State Legitimacy or Promoting Change?" In *The*

Changing Politics of Non-Governmental Organizations and African States, ed. Eva Sandberg. Westport, CT: Praeger, 1994.

Johnson, Richard L., and Eric Ledbetter. " 'Spiritualizing the Political': Christ and Christianity in Gandhi's Satyagraha." *Peace and Change* 22 (1) (January 1997): 32–47.

Johnson, Walston. "The Africanization of a Mission Church: The African Methodist Episcopal Church in Zambia." In *African Christianity: Patterns of Religious Continuity*, ed. George Bond et al. New York: Academic Press, 1979.

Johnstone, Douglas, and Cynthia Samson. *Religion: The Missing Dimension of Statecraft*. New York: Oxford University Press, 1994.

Johnstone, Patrick. *Operation World: The Day by Day Guide to Praying for the World*. Grand Rapids, MI: Zondervan Publishing House, 1993.

Joseph, Richard. "The Christian Churches and Democracy in Contemporary Africa." In *Christianity and Democracy in Global Context*, ed. Joseph Witte. Boulder, CO: Westview Press, 1993.

Juckes, Tim J. *Opposition in Southern Africa: The Leadership of Z. K. Mathews, Nelson Mandela, and Stephen Biko*. Westport, CT: Praeger, 1995.

Kapungu, Leonard. *Rhodesia: The Struggle for Freedom*. New York: Orbis Books, 1974.

Karis, Thomas, and Gwendolen M. Carter. *From Protest to Challenge: A Documentary History of African Politics in South Africa 1882–1964*. Vols. 1–4. Stanford, CA: Hoover Institution Press, 1978.

Kasozi, A.B.K. "Christian-Muslim Inputs into Public Formation in Kenya, Tanzania and Uganda." In *Religion and Politics in East Africa*, ed. Holger Bernt Hansen and Michael Twaddle. Athens: Ohio University Press, 1995.

Kastfelt, Niels. *Religion and Politics in Nigeria: A Study in Middle Belt Christianity*. New York: British Academic Press, 1994.

Katjavivi, Peter H., et al., ed. *Church and Liberation in Namibia*. London: Pluto Press, 1989.

Kaunda, Kenneth D. *A Humanist in Africa: Letters to Colin M. Morris from Kenneth D. Kaunda*, Nashville: Abingdon Press, 1966.

———. *Zambia Shall Be Free. An Autobiography*. New York: Praeger, 1963.

Keller, Bill. "Mugabe Finds Useful Target in White Farmlands: Expropriation Threat." *New York Times* (22 August 1993), 2.

Kempton, Daniel. *Soviet Strategy toward African National Liberation Movements*. New York: Praeger, 1989.

Kinghorn, Johann. "The Theology of Separate Equality: A Critical Outline of the DRC's Position on Apartheid." In *Christianity amidst Apartheid: Selected Perspectives on the Church in South Africa*, ed. Martin Prozeky. New York: St. Martin's Press, 1990.

Kobia, Samuel. "Promoting Democracy in Africa: Experiences and Future Perspectives." *Church and Society.* (March–April, 1995): 13–29.

Kokole, Omari H. "Idi Amin, 'the Nubi' and Islam in Ugandan Politics 1971–1979." In *Religion and Politics in East Africa*, ed. Holger Bernt Hansen and Michael Twaddle. Athens: Ohio University Press, 1995.

Laguma, Alex. *Apartheid.* New York: International Publishers, 1971.

Lamarchand, Rene. "Review Essay: The Africanist as Intellectual: A Note on Jean-Francois Bayart." *African Studies Review* 35 (April 1992): 129–133.

Lamola, John M. "Change Is Pain: A Projective Reflection on the Mission of the Church in South Africa beyond 1994." *International Review of Mission* (01 January 1994): 37–44.

Lapsley, Michael. "Anglican Church and State from UDI in 1965 until the Independence of Zimbabwe in 1980." In *Church and State in Zimbabwe*, ed. Carl F. Hallencreutz, and Ambrose M. Moyo. Harare: Mambo Press, 1988.

Levine, Daniel H., ed. *Religion and Political Conflict in Latin America.* Chapel Hill: University of North Carolina Press, 1986.

Lewis, Peter M. "Political Transition and the Dilemma of Civil Society in Africa." *Journal of International Affairs* 46 (1) (Summer 1992): 31–54.

Leys, Colin, and John S. Saul, eds. *Namibia's Liberation Struggle: The Two-Edged Sword.* Athens: Ohio University Press, 1995.

Linden, Ian. "The Roman Catholic Church in Social Crisis: The Case of Rwanda." In *Christianity in Independent Africa*, ed. Edward Fashole-Luke et al. Bloomington: Indiana University Press, 1978.

———. *The Catholic Church and the Struggle for Zimbabwe.* London: Longman, 1980.

Lipjhart, Arend. "Comparative Politics and the Comparative Method." *Comparative Politics: Notes and Readings*, ed. Roy Macridis and Bernard E. Brown. Homewood, IL: Dorsey Press, 1988.

Lonsdale, John, et al. "The Emerging Patterns of Church State Co-operation in Kenya." In *Christianity in Independent Africa*, ed. Edward Fashole-Luke et al. Bloomington: University of Indiana Press, 1978.

Lotter, H.P.P. "Religion and Politics in Transforming South Africa." *Journal of the Church and State* 34 (3) (Summer 1992): 475–502.

Lovgren, Stefan. "It Takes a Dictatorship to Raise a Democracy." *US News and World Report* (23 March 1998), 41.

Luthuli, Albert. *Africa's Freedom.* London: Unwin Books, 1964.

MacGaffey, Wyatt. "Religion, Class and Social Pluralism in Zaire." In *Religions, State and Society in Contemporary Africa: Niger, Sudan, South Africa, Zaire and Mozambique*, Austin Ahanotu, New York: Peter Lang, 1992.

Macridis, Roy, and Bernard E. Brown, eds. *Comparative Politics: Notes and Readings.* Homewood, IL: Dorsey Press, 1970.

Majaju, Akiiki B. "The Political Crisis of Church Institutions in Uganda." *African Affairs* 75 (298) (January 1976): 67–85.

Maritz, Frans. "Church-State Relations in the Dutch Reformed Church (NGK) in Zimbabwe: A Case Study." In *Church and State in Zimbabwe*, ed. Carl F. Hallencreutz and Ambrose M. Moyo. Harare: Mambo Press, 1988.

Mathews, Arthur H. "Terror and Death in Uganda." *Christianity Today* (18 March 1977), 49–51.

Maylam, Paul. *A History of the African People of South Africa: From the Early Iron Age to the 1970s.* New York: St. Martin's Press, 1986.

McDonagh, Enda. *Church and Politics: From Theology to a Case History of Zimbabwe.* Notre Dame, IN: University of Notre Dame Press, 1980.

McLaughlin, Janice. " 'We Did It for Love': Refugees and Religion in the Camps in Mozambique and Zambia during Zimbabwe's Liberation Struggle." In *Church and State in Zimbabwe*, ed. Carl F. Hallencreutz and Ambrose M. Moyo. Harare: Mambo Press, 1988.

Men, Mathew C., and Lowell S. Gustafson, eds. *The Religious Challenge to the State.* Philadelphia: Temple University Press, 1992.

Meyns, Peter, and Dani Wadada, eds. *Democracy and the One-Party State in Africa.* Hamburg, Germany: Instut fur Afrika-Kunde, 1989.

Mfoulu, Jean. "The Catholic Church and Camerian Nationalism." In *Christianity in Independent Africa*, ed. Edward Fashole-Luke et al. Bloomington: University of Indiana Press, 1978.

Miller, Marlin E., and Barbara Nelson Gingerich. *The Church's Peace Witness.* Grand Rapids, MI: Eerdmans, 1994.

Mofokeng, Takatso. "Black Theology in South Africa: Achievements, Problems and Prospects." In *Christianity amidst Apartheid*, ed. Martin Prozesky. New York: St. Martin's Press, 1990.

Molebatsi, Caesar, and David Virtue. *A Flame for Justice: The Man Whose Heart Burns for the Youth of Soweto—the Citizens of South Africa's Tomorrow.* London: Lion Publishing, 1991.

Morris, Colin M. *The End of the Missionary: A Short Account of the Political Consequences of a Missionary in Northern Rhodesia.* London: Cargate Press, 1962.

Mulford, David C. *Zambia: The Politics of Independence 1957–1964.* New York: Oxford University Press, 1967.

Mushete, Ngindu. "Christianity and Authenticity in Zaire," In *Christianity in Independent Africa*, ed. Edward Fashole-Luke, et al. Bloomington: Indiana University Press, 1978.

Mutambirwa, James A. Chamunorewa. *The Rise of Settler Power in Southern Rhodesia (Zimbabwe), 1898–1923.* Toronto: Associated University Press, 1980.

Muzorewa, Abel. "The Role of the ANC." In *Zimbabwe Now*. London: Rex Collins, 1972.

———. *Rise up and Walk: The Autobiography of Bishop Tendekar Muzorewa*, ed. Norman E. Thomas. Nashville, TN: Abingdon, 1978.

Mwanakatwe, John. *End of Kaunda Era*. Lusaka: Multimedia Publications, 1994.

Ncozana, Silas. "The Church's Engagement With Political and Social Issues: The Perspective of the Church in Malawi." *Church and Society*. (March–April, 1995): 31–37.

Nkiwane, Solomon M. *The Churches' Roles as Agents of Peace and Development: Case Study—Zimbabwe*. Uppsala, Sweden: Life and Peace Institute, 1992.

Nurnberger, Klaus. "The Task of the Church concerning the Economy in a Post-apartheid South Africa." *Missionalia* 22, no. 7 (August 1994): 118–146.

O'Brien, Donal B. Cruise. "Coping with the Christians: The Muslim Predicament in Kenya." In *Religion and Politics in East Africa*, ed. Holger Bernt Hansen and Michael Twaddle. Athens: Ohio University Press, 1995.

Odendaal, Andre. *Black Protest Politics in South Africa to 1912*. Totowa, NJ: Barnes and Noble Books, 1984.

O'Fahey, R. S. "The Past in the Present? The Issue of the Sharia in Sudan." In *Religion and Politics in East Africa*, ed. Holger Bernt Hansen and Michael Twaddle. Athens: Ohio University Press, 1995.

Paeden, Roger. "The Contribution of the Epworth Mission Settlement to African Development." In *Themes in the Christian History of Central Africa*, ed. Terence Ranger and John Weller. Los Angeles: University of California Press, 1975.

Panter-Brick, Keith. "Prospects for Democracy in Zambia." *Government and Opposition* 29 (2) (Spring 1994): 231–247.

Parker, Roger. "A Tangled Revolution." *Commonweal* 113 (28 February 1986): 107–110.

Pattnayak, Satya R., ed. *Organized Religion in the Political Transformation of Latin America*. New York: University Press of America, 1995.

Phiri, Isaac. "Poll Drive a Mixed Success." *African Concord* (17 December 1987).

———. "Zambians Must Now Pay for Education and Health" *Compass News Features* (London) (14 July 1989).

———. "Testing Time for Kaunda." *Compass News Features* (London) (15 January 1991).

———. "Gulf War: Kaunda's Baghdad Connection." *Compass News Features* (London) (22 February 1991).

———. "Is the End Coming for Kaunda?" *Compass News Features* (London) (11 July 1991).

————. "Zambia's Traditional Rulers Face Challenge of Democracy." *Compass News Features* (London) (16 July 1991).

————. "Evangelical Wins Peaceful Election." *Christianity Today* (16 December 1991), 70.

————. "We Have Been Creating a Culture of Violence." *World Evangelical Fellowship* (15 February 1993): 12–13.

————. "Evangelical President Contends with Corruption, Economy Woes." *Christianity Today* (3 April 1995), 94.

————. "The Making of a Christian Nation: An Interview with President Chiluba of Zambia." *Today* (South Africa) (July/August, 1995): 14–16.

————. "Chiluba's Christian Nation." *On Being* (Australia) (8 September 1995): 20–21.

————. "President Disappoints Christians." *Christianity Today* (2 March 1998), 76–77.

————. "Publish for Africa's Hope and Future." *Interlit: The International Magazine of Christian Publishing* (April 1998): 6–7.

————. *Carter and Africa: Pre-presidential to Post-presidential Years*. Atlanta: Mercer University Press, forthcoming.

Pollard, Alton B. "The Dawn of Freedom: A South Africa Diary," *Africa Today* 41 (1) (1994): 58–64.

Prozesky, Martin, ed. *Christianity amidst Apartheid: Selected Perspectives on the Church in South Africa*. New York: St Martin's Press, 1990.

Przeworski, Adam, and Henry Tuene. *The Logic of Comparative Social Inquiry*. New York: Wiley-Interscience, 1970.

Raeburn, Michael. *Black Fire: Accounts of the Guerilla War in Rhodesia*. London: Julian Friedmann Publishers, 1978.

Ranger, Terence. *The African Voice in Southern Rhodesia 1989–1930*. Evanston IL: Northwestern University Press, 1970.

————. "The Churches, Nationalist State and African Religion." In *Christianity in Independent Africa,* ed. Edward Fashole-Luke, et al. Bloomington: Indiana University Press, 1978.

————. *Are We Not Also Men? The Samkange Family and African Politics in Zimbabwe 1920–64*. Portsmouth, NH: Heinemann, 1995.

Ranger, Terence, and John Weller, eds. *Themes in the Christian History of Central Africa*. Los Angeles: University of California Press, 1975.

Rosberg, Carl G., and Thomas M. Callaghy, eds. *Socialism in Sub-Saharan Africa: A New Assessment*. Berkeley, CA: Institute of International Studies, 1979.

Rossow, G. J., and Eugenio Macamo. "Church-State Relationships in Mozambique." *Journal of Church and State* 35 (Summer 1993).

Rotberg, I. Robert. *Christian Missionaries and the Creation of Northern Rhodesia 1880–1924*. Princeton, NJ: Princeton University Press, 1965.

Rotberg, I. Robert and A. Mazrui. *Protest and Power in Black Africa*. New York: Oxford University Press, 1970.

Saayem, Willem. In *Christianity amidst Apartheid: Selected Perspectives on the Church in South Africa*, ed. Martin Prozesky. New York: St. Martin's Press, 1990.

Samkange, Stanlake. *Origins of Rhodesia*. New York: Praeger, 1969.

Sandberg, Eve, ed. *The Changing Politics of Non-Governmental Organizations in African States*. Wesport, CT: Praeger, 1994.

Santa Ana, Julio de. "The Concept of Civil Society." *The Ecumenical Review* 46 (1) (January 1994): 3–11.

Saul, John S. ed. *A Difficult Road: The Transition to Socialism in Mozambique*. New York: Monthly Review Press, 1985.

Schatzberg, Michael G. *The Dialects of Oppression in Zaire*. Bloomington: Indiana University Press, 1988.

Seekings, Jeremy. "Trailing behind Masses: The United Democratic Front and Township in the Pretoria-Witersrand-Vaal Region, 1983–84." *Journal of Southern African Studies* 18, 1 (99–114) (March 1992): 114.

Sempangi, F. Kefa. "Uganda's Reign of Terror." *World View* 5 (5 May 1975): 16–21.

Shupe, Anson, and Jeffrey K. Hadden, eds. *The Politics of Religion and Social Change*. New York: Paragon House, 1988.

Sindima, Harvey. *Religious and Political Ethics in Africa: A Moral Inquiry*. Westport, CT: Greenwood Press, 1998.

Steele, Murray. " 'With Hope Unconquered . . . ': Arthur Shearly Cripps, 1869–1952." In *Themes in the Christian History of Central Africa*, ed. Terence Ranger and John Weller. Los Angeles: University of California Press, 1975.

Steenkamp, Philip. "The Churches." In *Namibia's Liberation Struggle: The Two-Edged Sword*, ed. Colin Leys and John S. Saul. Athens: Ohio University Press, 1995.

Taylor, John V. *Christianity and Politics in Africa*. London: Penguin, 1957.

Taylor, John V., and Dorothea A. Lehmann. *Christians of the Copperbelt: The Growth of the Church in Northern Rhodesia*. London: SCM Press Ltd., 1962.

Temple, Arnold. "Should the Church Meddle in Politics?" *Mindolo World* 2 (1991): 8–12.

Tetzlaff, Rainer. "The Social Basis of Political Rule in Africa: Problems of Legitimacy and Prospects for Democracy." In *Democracy and the One-Party State in Africa*, ed. Peter Meyns and Dani Wadada. Hamburg, Germany: Insitut fur Afrika-Kunde, 1989.

Thomas, Linda E. "African Indigenous Churches as a Source of Socio-Political Transformation in South Africa." *Africa Today* 41 (1994): 39–56.

Throup, David. " 'Render unto Caesar the Things That Are Caesar's': The Politics of Church-State Conflict in Kenya 1978–1990." In *Religion and Politics in East Africa*, ed. Holger Bernt Hansen and Michael Twaddle. Athens: Ohio University Press, 1995.

Tinder, Glenn. *The Political Meaning of Christianity*. New York: HarperCollins, 1991.

Tutu, Desmond. *Crying in the Wilderness*. London: Mowbray, 1986.

———. "To be Human is to be Free." In *Christianity and Democracy in Global Context*, ed. John Witte Jr. Boulder, CO: Westview Press, 1993.

Tutu, Naomi. *The Words of Desmond Tutu: Selected by Naomi Tutu*. New York: Newmarket Press, 1989.

Twaddle, Michael. "Was the Democratic Party of Uganda Purely a Confessional Party?" In *Christianity in Independent Africa*, ed. Edward Fashole-Luke et al. Bloomington: University of Indiana Press, 1978.

U.S. Congress. Senate Committee on Foreign Relations. A Rhodesian Settlement? Analysis of an African Agreement Signed by Prime Minister Ian Smith of Rhodesia, the Reverend Ndabaningi Sithole, Bishop Abel Muzorewa and Senator Jeremiah Chirau on March 3, 1978. A Staff Report to the Committee on Foreign Relations, 95th Congress, June 1978.

Villa-Vicencio, Charles. *Trapped in Apartheid: A Socio-Theological History of the English-Speaking Churches*. New York: Orbis Books, 1988.

———. "When Violence Begets Violence: Is the Armed Struggle Justified." In *Christianity amidst Apartheid: Selected Perspectives on the Church in South Africa*, ed. Martin Prozesky. New York: St. Martin's Press, 1990.

Voll, John O. "Religion and Politics in Islamic Africa." In *The Religious Challenge to the State*, ed. Mathew C. Men, and Lowell S. Gustafson. Philadelphia: Temple University Press, 1992.

Wald, Kenneth D. *Religion and Politics in the United States*. New York: St Martin's Press, 1987.

Waldeck, Val. "The Day God Saved South Africa." *Christian Reader* (March/April 1996): 82–89.

Waliggo, John Mary. "The Catholic Church and the Root Cause of Political Instability in Uganda." In *Religion and Politics in East Africa*, ed. Holger Bernt Hansen and Michael Twaddle. Athens: Ohio University Press, 1995.

———. *Church versus State in South Africa: The Case of the Christian Institute*. New York: Orbis Books, 1983.

Ward, Kevin. "The Church of Uganda amidst Conflict: The Interplay between Church and Politics in Uganda since 1962." In *Religion and Politics in East Africa*, ed. Holger Bernt Hansen and Michael Twaddle. Athens: Ohio University Press, 1995.

Water, Desmond Van Der. "Born out of Unity and for Unity: The Witness of the United Congregational Church of Southern Africa in South Africa." *International Review of Mission* (01 January 1994): 159–162.

Weigle, Marcia A., and Jim Butterfield. "Civil Society in Reforming Communists: The Logic of Emergence," *Comparative Politics* 21 (4) (1992): 1–23.

Weller, John. "The Influence on National Affairs of Alison May, Bishop of Northern Rhodesia, 1914–40." In *Themes in the Christian History of Central Africa*, ed. Terence Ranger, and John Weller. Los Angeles: University of California Press, 1975.

Westerlund, David. "Secularism, Civil Religion, or Islam? Islamic Revivalism and the National Question in Nigeria." In *Religion, State and Society in Contemporary Africa*, ed. Austin Ahanotu. New York: Peter Lang, 1992.

Wiarda, Howard J. *Introduction to Comparative Politics: Concepts and Processes*. Belmont, CA: Wadsworth, 1993.

Wiseman, Henry, and Alistair M. Taylor. *From Rhodesia to Zimbabwe: The Politics of Transition*. New York: Pergamon Press, 1981.

Witte, John Jr., ed. *Christianity and Democracy in Global Context*. Boulder, CO: Westview Press, 1993.

Woods, Donald. *Biko*. New York: Vintage Books, 1979.

Woudberg, Neville. "Michael Cassidy Letter Appeals for Reconciliation." *World Evangelical Report* (15 October 1993).

Yarnold, Barbara, ed. *The Role of Religious Organizations in Social Movements*. New York: Praeger, 1991.

Young, Crawford. *The African Colonial State in Comparative Perspective*. New Haven, CT: Yale University Press, 1994.

Young, Crawford, and Thomas Turner. *The Rise and Decline of the Zairian State*. Madison: University of Wisconsin Press, 1985.

Young, Kenneth. *Rhodesia and Independence*. New York: James Heinemann, 1967.

Zambia Episcopal Conference. *Economics, Politics and Justice: Statement of the Catholic Bishops of Zambia, 1990*. Lusaka: Zambia Episcopal Conference, 1990.

Zimbabwe Now. London: Rex Collins, 1972.

Zvobgo, Chengai J. "The African Franchise Question." In *Church and State in Zimbabwe*, ed. Carl F. Hallencreutz and Ambrose M. Moyo. Harare: Mambo Press, 1988.

Index

About the Author

ISAAC PHIRI is director of international training for Cook Communications, a not-for-profit organization that promotes indigenous publishing around the world. He is also adjunct professor of social science in the Master of Liberal Studies program at Regis University in Colorado. He has written numerous journal and magazine articles and book chapters.

ELIAS MUNSHYA
Barrister & Solicitor